Dedication

Dedicated to my sister, Amy, for being such a fun person to be around.

Credits

Publisher
Lloyd J. Short

Associate Publisher
Rick Ranucci

Publishing Manager
Joseph B. Wikert

Production Editor
Kezia Endsley

Technical Editors
Greg Guntle
Jay Munro

Editorial Assistants
Elizabeth D. Brown
Stacey Beheler

Production Manager
Corinne Walls

Proofreading/Indexing Coordinator
Joelynn Gifford

Production Analyst
Mary Beth Wakefield

Book Designer
Scott Cook

Cover Designer
Jay Corpus

Graphic Image Specialists
Dennis Sheehan
Jerry Ellis
Susan VandeWalle

Production
Debra Adams
Jeff Baker
Claudia Bell
Julie Brown
Paula Carroll
Brad Chinn
Tim Cox
Mark Enochs
Bob LaRoche
Jay Lesandrini
Tom Loveman
Linda Seifert
Sandra Shay
Marcella Thompson

Indexer
Johnna VanHoose

[redacted]

Crash Course in C

Paul J. Perry

PROGRAMMING
SERIES

que

[redacted]

Crash Course in C

Library of Congress Catalog No.: 92-81763

ISBN: 1-56529-149-2

96 95 94 93 8 7 6 5 4 3 2 1

Interpretation of the printing code: the rightmost double-digit number is the year of the book's printing; the rightmost single-digit number, the number of the book's printing. For example, a printing code of 93-1 shows that the first printing of the book occurred in 1993.

Trademarks

Composed in *ITC Garamond* and *MCPdigital*
by Prentice Hall Computer Publishing.

About the Author

Paul J. Perry

Paul J. Perry works at a major software vendor where he specializes in programming in C and C++. He has been programming in C since 1987. Mr. Perry is the author of *Using Turbo Pascal for Windows* (Que), *Do It Yourself Turbo C++* (Sams), and *DESQView Instant Reference* (Sybex). If he is not writing or programming, you will find him on his bicycle riding 15 to 25 miles per day.

Acknowledgments

Thanks to the fabulous team at Que, including Joseph Wikert, Kezia Endsley, Greg Guntle, and all the other people behind the scenes. It could not have been done without you.

Contents at a Glance

Table of Contents

Introduction

The C programming language is used by most major software developers in writing the vast majority of their applications. C has quickly become the most popular and powerful programming language in existence.

Virtually all the current books about C programming are large, comprehensive books that explore every aspect of the language. I took a different approach with this book. This book teaches only the essential elements of C programming. *Crash Course in C* offers the reader the *fastest* way to learn the C programming language.

This book takes a "no-frills" approach to teaching the most important aspects of the C language. You start learning C in the first chapter. This book focuses on the key features of the language. It enables you to begin writing practical applications in the shortest amount of time possible.

Who Should Use This Book?

This book is aimed at readers who want to learn the C programming language in the shortest amount of time possible. The audience includes non-programmers who can learn in a fast-track environment as well as programmers who are switching to C.

What You Should Know to Use This Book

This book assumes that you are familiar with common computer terminology. Time is not wasted teaching you what an ASCII code is or how to write a batch file to start a C compiler. You should have a good grasp of basic computing principles before reading this book.

Although programming experience is not necessary, it is helpful if you have programmed (even a little) in some computer language. Whether you have worked with FORTRAN, BASIC, or Pascal, the knowledge you already have helps you in getting up to speed in C.

Organization of This Book

Crash Course in C is divided into 11 chapters. Each chapter covers a fundamental aspect of the language. You start with programming basics and move to every essential element of C programming. Table I.1 summarizes the contents of each chapter.

Table I.1. Organization of *Crash Course in C*.

Chapter	*Contents*
1	History and basic structure of C language.
2	Example program, explained step by step.
3	Description and purpose of C variables and operators.
4	How to get keyboard input and display video output.
5	An examination of decision-making statements.
6	Discussion of C's looping statements.
7	Explanation of functions and how they are used.
8	Description of C's preprocessor directives.
9	Information about pointers and other data types.
10	How to use advanced data structures.
11	How to access disk files in C.

By the end of this book, you will be familiar with the important concepts of C programming and will be able to speak knowledgeably about the subject. This will lead you to being able to create programs in C.

Notation and Conventions

To get the most out of this book, you should know how it is designed. New terms and emphasized words are presented in *italicized text* and are defined on first reference. Pay close attention to italicized text. Functions, commands, parameters, and the like are set in `monospace` text; for example, the `main()` function. User responses that must be typed at the prompt appear in **`monospace bold`**; for example:

```
Please Enter Your Name: Kevin
```

Placeholders (words that you replace with actual values) in code lines appear in *`monospace italic`*; for example:

```
long double variable1, variable2;
```

In this example, you would replace *`variable1`* and *`variable2`* with the appropriate numbers, depending, of course, on the program you were writing.

Full C programs appear as listings with listing heads, whereas code fragments appear alone within the text. This book covers all C compilers that support the ANSI C standard. Therefore, no matter what operating system or compiler you are using, the examples should compile and enable you to get hands-on experience in C programming.

Throughout the book, you will also see *Syntax-at-a-Glance* shaded boxes with the syntax icon. This design feature provides easy language reference to the essential elements of C programming. By providing this helpful information, the book will serve not only as a tutorial, but as a reference that will serve you for a long time to come.

Syntax at a Glance

The Syntax-at-a-Glance Box

This is a Syntax-at-a-Glance box. It provides syntax explanations for C functions and procedures. You can use this information time and time again as a quick reference to the C language syntax.

The box first provides you with the standard format of the function or procedure, like so:

```
standard function (goes here);
```

A few examples generally follow, like so:

```
standard function (get)
standard function (put)
standard function (if)
```

For more information regarding the function, read the text surrounding the box.

Other visual pointers found in this book include:

CAUTION

Caution boxes that warn you of problem areas, including possible cases in which you might introduce bugs into your program or crash your system.

and

NOTE

Note boxes that provide you with extraneous information. Many times, this information will help speed your learning process and provide you with shortcuts in C. Other times, it simply reminds you of information important enough to be mentioned twice!

Learn by Doing

There is an important rule about programming. ***You learn by doing!*** Trying an example is one of the best ways to learn. It is impossible to learn C without writing code, compiling your programs, and observing the way they work.

Because practicing programming is essential to learning the C language, example programs are included for you to try. However, I urge you to try your own examples as well. It is imperative to experiment with a language to really learn it, and C is no exception.

So, with all this out of the way, you can begin your journey of C programming.

CHAPTER ONE

C Programming Basics

Introduction to C

C is a general-purpose, structured programming language that can be used for a broad variety of programming tasks. The C language is characterized by its capability to produce concise source code programs. This is, in part, due to the large number of *operators* (symbols that cause a program to do something to its variables) included in the language. Furthermore, most implementations of the language have a rather extensive library of *functions* (sections of code that perform specific tasks) that enhance the basic language definition.

C resembles other high-level structured programming languages such as Pascal and Modula-2; however, C contains features that enable programmers to use it at a lower level as well. In this way, it bridges the gap between machine language and high-level structured languages.

History of C

C was originally designed and implemented in 1972 by Dennis Ritchie at Bell Telephone Laboratories, Inc. (now AT&T Bell Laboratories), and outlined in the book *The C Programming Language,* by Brian Kernighan and Dennis Ritchie. C was an outgrowth of two earlier languages—BCPL and B—also developed at Bell Laboratories.

Although C is now used on many different computer systems, it was first associated with the UNIX operating system because UNIX was written with the C programming language. For this reason and its general usefulness in developing operating systems, the language has sometimes been called a "system programming language." C combines high-level language constructions with the capability to interact with the operating system at a low level.

As developers began programming in C, different dialects of the language started appearing on different computing platforms. Because parts of the language weren't clearly defined, they were interpreted differently by each compiler implementation. It was clear that C needed to be updated so an industry standard could be established.

In 1983, the *American National Standards Institute* (ANSI) established a committee to create a standard definition of the C programming language. The committee included professors, researchers, and programmers from some of the top computer companies. In 1988, the second edition of the book by Kernighan and Ritchie (by this time known as K&R) was published. It included the standardized version of C, called *ANSI C.*

Types of C Compilers

All modern C *compilers* (programs that convert the C language into instructions that are executed by the microprocessor) support the ANSI standard version of C. Many compilers also provide additional language enhancements. These enhancements are either dependent on the computer on which they are being used or are additions to the language that make C easier to use.

If you purchase a compiler from Borland International or Microsoft Corporation, you receive special *compiler extensions* that make C easier to use on PC-based systems. These compilers almost always have an option that disables any compiler extensions, making C compile the code only in accordance with ANSI specifications. For the examples in this book, you might want to do this.

When you program in accordance with the ANSI standard, your code is *portable* to other operating systems. (This means the code can run with little or no modification on different systems.) This is a valuable characteristic because as you program, you need to be able to use your application on different computer systems. Doing so opens up large markets for your software. The less hassle and time it takes when converting your code to different systems, the more time you can spend adding functionality to your program— or vacationing in Tahiti.

Today, many vendors are beginning to sell *C++* compilers. The C++ language is a *superset* of C. This means that programs written in C++ have all the features of C, plus more. The fact of the matter is that you must know C before you can start learning C++. Therefore, if you buy a C++ compiler, you can still compile C programs. Furthermore, you have the ability to move on to C++ and object-oriented programming in the future, as your needs expand.

NOTE Don't be scared about buying a C++ compiler. The C++ compiler suits all your needs and provides more features for the future.

Why Code in C?

There must be some reasons for the popularity of C. Although C can be difficult to use, it also has many strong points. As you begin using C, you will recognize many of the following virtues:

- C is often called a *middle-level language.* The C programming language is a middle-level language because it combines elements of high-level languages (such as Pascal and FORTRAN) with functions of assembly language (the capability to work at the lowest level of the computer). This is important because it enables you to work with an easy-to-understand language, and still accomplish tasks that could previously only be done with cryptic instructions to the microprocessor.
- The C programming language incorporates many design features that make it a natural language for computer programming.
- The C programming language is a *structured language.* The idea of a structured language is that you can break your code into small chunks and put each chunk of code into its own subprogram (or function). Your main program is then made up of multiple subprograms. Each subprogram has its own logic and is a program in itself. This is valuable because a structured programming language enables you to create large-scale programs that can be easily understood.

- The way that the C programming language enables you to program makes C an efficient language in which to code. Programs in C can be written in several lines, whereas other languages might consume half a page to accomplish the same task (assuming the task can be done in the other language).

- Programs written in C are *portable.* As stated earlier, this means that C programs written on one system can run with little or no modification on other systems. Compilers for C are available on just about every operating system. Everything from personal computers to mainframe machines now have C compilers.

- The C programming language is powerful and flexible. An operating system is one of the most fundamental programs ever written and C was developed with this operating-system development in mind. C is not meant to be easy to read or simple to understand. Its sole purpose is to enable the programmer to have access to all levels of the computer.

Although there are probably other reasons that make C popular, these are the most common. If you ever become discouraged while learning C, remember that word processors, spreadsheets, arcade-style games, and operating systems all have been written in C. If these other programmers were able to learn C, you will be able to also.

Now that you have an idea about the history and benefits of C, you are ready to learn about the differences between compiled and interpreted languages.

Compiled and Interpreted Languages

If your programming experience has been limited to BASIC, you might find some of the operations of C rather strange. Program development tools are divided into two broad categories: *interpreted* and *compiled* languages. BASIC is an interpreted language, whereas C is a compiled language.

A program written in a high-level language must be translated into machine language before it can be executed. *Compilers* (such as C and Pascal) translate an entire program into machine language before executing any of the instructions. *Interpreters* (which is how the BASIC language is usually implemented) proceed through a program by first translating each line and then executing the instructions, one instruction at a time—slowly making their way through the program.

A compiler or interpreter is a computer program that accepts a high-level program (such as a C program) as input and generates a corresponding machine-language program as output. The original high-level program is called the *source code*, and the resulting machine-language program is called the *object code*. Another program combines the object code and creates an executable file. This process is known as *linking*. See Figure 1.1 for a visual representation of these processes.

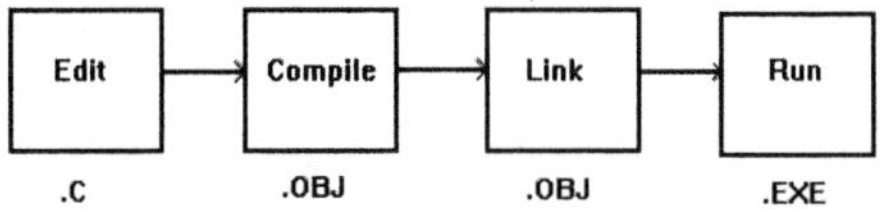

Figure 1.1. *The processes of editing, compiling, linking, and running your programs.*

Every high-level language must have a compiler or interpreter. If you have used GW-BASIC, BASICA, or QBASIC, you have used an interpreter. Most implementations of C operate as compilers. Pascal and FORTRAN are also compiled languages. Several languages have versions of interpreters and compilers available for them.

Interpreted languages are usually more convenient to use during program development. However, once a program is error-free, a compiled version of the program executes much faster than an interpreted version. Most important, the compiled version of the program only has to be accompanied by the resulting machine-language program since your source code was not distributed.

An interpreted language requires that you distribute the (usually proprietary) source code of the program and also requires that the language interpreter be present at runtime to interpret the code.

Program Creation In C

Although the exact steps you follow to create a program in C depend on the compiler and operating system you are using, there are certain procedures that always must be followed.

The most commonly used operating system for program development in C is the PC- or UNIX-based systems. You will read about some of the details of these systems after you learn about the overall program-creation process.

Writing the Code

When you write a program in C, you first use an editor to store the text of the program into an ASCII text file. This text file is referred to as the program's *source file.* The first part of the filename, the *prefix*, describes the purpose or contents of the program (for example, MYPROG). On PC-based systems, you are limited to eight characters for each filename prefix. Other operating systems provide more characters.

In most cases, you also give C source files a filename with the extension (or *suffix*) of .C. This reminds the compiler (and you) that the file comprises C source code. The results are filenames like HELLO.C, FIRST.C, and MYPROG.C.

Compiling the Program

Now that you have a program's source code file, the next action you are most likely to take is to execute the file. In order to do this, you must first compile the file. The compiler converts your source code to an intermediate file, called the *object module.*

After you compile the program, the object module file is created. The *object module* is an intermediate file with an .OBJ extension (or suffix). The object module is simply a form of assembly language. However, there are several things missing from the object module. First, any library functions that your program calls are not included in this file. Second, the code that begins the program, called the *start-up code*, is not included in the object module.

Although the object module contains assembly language, it is not ready to be executed. To execute the file, it must be combined with the start-up code and the library functions that your program uses. Doing so will create a program file.

Linking Your Code

The linking process combines your .OBJ file with the start-up code and library functions into a final program. The final program has an extension of .EXE on PC-based computers. Other systems may have different file extensions.

Running the File

You can run the executable file by typing its filename at the command-line prompt. At that point, you see the fruits of your labor.

Although this might seem like a difficult process, it is actually rather simple. The reason for its simplicity is that modern C compilers have *streamlined* this process.

For example, compilers from Borland International contain an *Integrated Development Environment* (IDE) that includes a built-in editor, compiler, and linker. This way, you can use the editor to write your source code. You can then make a selection from a menu and your program is compiled into an object module, linked into a final .EXE, and executed, all in one simple step.

As you might guess, the Integrated Development Environment (IDE) has helped the productivity of programmers by making program development much easier. It reduces the time necessary to manually compile, link, and execute a program.

Debugging and Testing Your Program

If you have programmed before, you know that many programs don't run the first time you execute them. The process of getting your program to run is known as *debugging*.

CAUTION

Even if you have a running program, you must test it to make sure it works as you expected. On simple programs, this can be as easy as executing it once and making sure the results are acceptable.

Debugging larger programs might require the help of others in order to test your program in a number of different situations. When a program goes into the testing stage, it is usually referred to as *beta testing*. Beta testing can be a valuable time-saver in program development because you receive feedback from people who are using your program on a daily basis and are doing real-life activities.

Summary

This chapter gave you a basis to understanding the C programming language. It gave you the history of C, the benefits of C, taught you about some of the types of C compilers available, introduced the concept of compiled and interpreted languages, and briefly explained the processes of editing, compiling, linking, running, and debugging a program written in C.

The following points were covered in this chapter:

- The *C Programming language* was developed by Brian Kernighan and Dennis Ritchie from AT&T Bell Labs.
- The *UNIX operating system* was written in C. Since then, C has been used on just about every major (and minor) operating system available.
- *ANSI C* is the standard definition of the language prepared by the American National Standards Institute. It provides a standard on which all C compilers can be based.
- Every program written in a high-level language must be translated into machine language before it can be executed. The two broad categories of software development tools are *interpreters* and *compilers.*
- In an *interpreted language,* the interpreter proceeds through a program by translating and then executing single instructions, one instruction at a time.
- In a compiled language, the high-level program instructions are called *source code,* the resulting machine-language program is executed when you want to run the program.
- In order to execute a program on your computer, you must first compile it. This creates an intermediate file called an *object module*. The object module is then linked with the compiler's libraries to create an executable program.

CHAPTER TWO

Your First Program

This chapter presents your first C program. You learn what each statement in the program does and how it relates to C programming in general. Each of the concepts covered in this chapter is described in more detail in later chapters. By the end of this chapter, you should begin to understand how C programming works.

Starting with an Example

Listing 2.1 presents your first C program. Take a quick look at the program. Use a text editor to create a source file by entering the listing into a text editor. Then compile, link, and run the program.

Listing 2.1. Your first C program.

```
/***************************************
 FIRST.C - Your first C program.
           Program to calculate the
           area of a circle.
 Crash Course in C by Paul J. Perry
 ***************************************/

#include <stdio.h>

#define PI 3.1415

int main()
{
   float area, radius;

   printf("Please Enter Radius: ");
   scanf("%f", &radius);
```

continues

Listing 2.1. Continued

```
   area = PI * radius * radius;

   printf("The Area is %f\n", area);

   return 0;
}
```

Listing 2.1 is an elementary C program that accepts the radius of a circle from the user, calculates the circle's area, then displays the calculated results.

When you run the program, it produces output similar to the following:

```
Please Enter Radius: 3
The Area is 28.273500
```

The user entered the **3** as the radius and the program provided the result. Take a look at each part of the program.

Learning the Elements of a C Program

The same basic components are necessary to create every C program. All C programs follow the same basic structure. Even a large, complex C program generally has the same layout as a short one. The following elements are found in most C programs:

- preprocessor directives
- variables
- declarations
- function declarations
- the `main()` function

Before you find out about the exact statements in the program, you should know a little bit about the general syntax of C.

Case Sensitivity

It is important to know that C is a case-sensitive language. This means that upper- and lowercase letters are treated as separate characters. For example, the names TOTAL, total, Total, and totaL are all treated as different identifiers. Languages such as BASIC and

Pascal, on the other hand, are not case-sensitive and treat these names in exactly the same way.

CAUTION

When you type a C program into the compiler, be careful to use the proper case. If you don't, the compiler will not recognize your code and the program will not be processed correctly.

The C Character Set

C uses the uppercase letters A to Z, the lowercase letters a to z, the digits 0 to 9, and the following special characters:

```
[    ]    {    }    <    >    (    )
!    *    +    =    "    '    .    ?
#    /    \    &    %    -    _    ^
~    |    ;    :    ,    @    $    `
```

C uses a combination of these characters to represent special operations. Some might be obvious (such as the addition (+) operator), others are not. They are defined in the book as they are introduced.

Using Comments in Your Program

Comments are an important part of any program. They help the person writing a program, and anyone else who must read the source file, to understand what's happening. All comments are ignored by the compiler, so they do not add to the size of the final executable program. Neither do they affect the execution time of the executable program.

A comment is not a required part of a program. It does not perform any programming task. Comments can be used freely throughout your program to make the code easier to understand.

In C, comments begin with the sequence `/*` and are terminated by the sequence `*/`. Everything within the markers is ignored. In the FIRST.C program, the first several lines of the program are comments, as follows:

```
/***************************************
 FIRST.C - Your first C program.
       Program to calculate the
       area of a circle.
 Crash Course in C by Paul J. Perry
 **************************************/
```

NOTE	Adding comments to your code is a valuable habit to adopt. When you look at old code, comments help refresh your memory as to the purpose of each section of code. Use comments throughout your code as much as possible. If there is ever a question in your mind as to whether to add a comment, always add it.

Helpful information to provide in the comments at the beginning of your program includes the author's name, the date the program was written, and any revision notes.

Including Preprocessor Directives

You can include various instructions to the C compiler in the source code of your program. These instructions are called *preprocessor directives.* Although they are not part of the C language, they expand the scope of C beyond its basic definition. All preprocessor directives begin with the pound (#) character.

The preprocessor directives are interpreted before the compilation process begins. Preprocessor directives usually appear at the beginning of a program and are grouped with other directives, although this is not required. The directives precede the code to which they refer.

The line in FIRST.C that follows instructs the compiler to include information about the standard input/output library:

```
#include <stdio.h>
```

This line appears at the beginning of many C source code files.

The `#include` directive instructs the compiler to include another source file in the file that contains the directive. The source file you want to include is enclosed in angle brackets. Figure 2.1 shows the effect of the `#include` directive.

In C, the file included in your code (in this case STDIO.H) is called the *header file,* or simply the *header.* The file has this name because declarations are usually found at the beginning of a program.

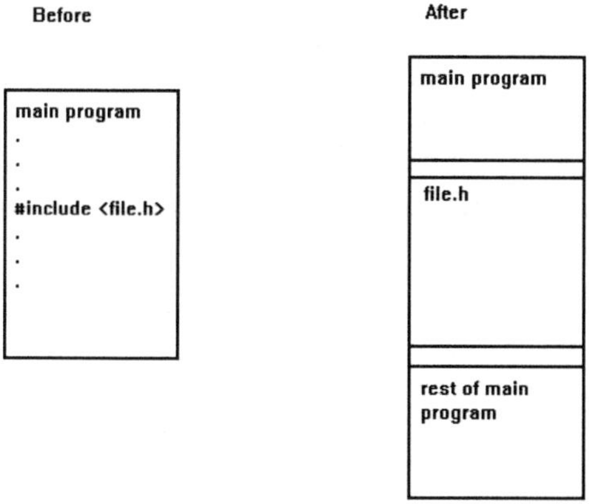

Figure 2.1. *The effect of adding the #include directive to your file.*

The other preprocessor directive in the FIRST.C program, as follows, is called a *definition statement:*

```
#define PI 3.1415
```

When the preprocessor scans the source code, it replaces all instances of `PI` with the number `3.1415`. This is a similar concept to a constant declaration.

Understanding the *main()* Function

Notice the `main()` function in Listing 2.1. The section of code starting with `main()` and enclosed in braces is called a *function.* Every C program consists of one or more functions, one of which must be called `main()`. Program execution always begins with the `main()` function.

NOTE The parentheses after the `main()` function inform the compiler that the program is calling a function. Even if a function does not pass any values to a function, `main()` still must have the empty parentheses.

All C programs are divided into small, separate units known as *functions.* Most high-level computer languages break programs into small units like this. Sometimes these smaller units are called *subprograms.*

FORTRAN and BASIC use subroutines. Pascal, being more similar to C, uses procedures and functions. There are obvious differences between how other languages operate, but the main idea of using the concept of functions is the same.

A C program is a collection of functions—each program is composed of one or more functions. Each function, then, contains one or more C statements. A function usually carries out a single task. Each function has a name and a list of values that the function receives. Most of the time, you can give a function any name you want. As you see shortly, the `main()` function is a special case.

A C program can have almost an unlimited number of functions. No matter how many functions exist, the `main()` function always receives control from the operating system when the program begins to run. All C programs must have a `main()` function because it is executed first every time your program begins to run.

Your program can have only one `main()` function. If you have more than one `main()`, the compiler does not know which to use. If you don't believe me, include more than one `main()` statement in your program and try to compile it. It won't work!

A *function definition* informs the compiler of the name of the function. When you learn more about functions, you will see that functions interact with values used in the program. In the FIRST.C program, the function definition is

```
int main()
```

The keyword `int` tells the compiler that the function returns an integer value. The word `main()` is the name of the function, and the parentheses tell the compiler that the programmer is creating the body of the function.

Some programs have only one function (like the one in Listing 2.1). Large programs have too much code to fit inside a single function. The large programs break tasks into logical steps, each of which is carried out in a function. Calls to the separate functions, then, are found inside `main()`.

Following the function definition are curly braces that signal the beginning and end of the function. The opening brace ({) signifies that a block of code is about to begin. The closing brace (}) terminates a block of code. In C, braces perform a similar function to the `Begin...End` statements in Pascal. In essence, braces mark the body of a function.

Learning the Parts of the Program

This section looks at the statements found inside the braces of the `main()` function. These statements are the code lines that actually compose the program.

Declaring Variables

Inside the `main()` function declaration you see a line that reads:

```
float area, radius;
```

This statement declares two floating-point variables. The names of the variables are `area` and `radius`. The keyword `float` signifies that the variables are to contain a decimal point. A variable is a symbolic name that can be assigned different values.

Displaying Output

To display text on the current output device (usually a video monitor), use a statement like this:

```
printf("Please Enter Radius: ");
```

This line is actually a call to another function. It is the formatted print or `printf()` function. The `printf()` function takes the argument passed to it—in this case a string constant—and outputs the argument to the standard output device. Because you included the STDIO.H file, which declares standard input and output functions, the string is displayed on the video monitor.

Getting Input

To get input from the user, use the `scanf()` function, as follows:

```
scanf("%f", &radius);
```

The `scanf()` function can be used to enter any combination of numerical values and single characters. This function returns the number of data items entered successfully.

When you call the `scanf()` function, you pass two parameters to it. The first is known as a *control string* and always appears inside quotation marks. The control string tells the compiler what types of numbers you want the user to enter. In this program, the `%f` refers to a floating-point number. The second parameter in the `scanf()` function specifies which variable should receive the value entered by the user.

The Meat of the Program

The main calculation of the program looks like this:

```
area = PI * radius * radius;
```

Remember that `PI` is actually a preprocessor directive that is replaced by a number. Thus, the line the compiler reads appears as so:

```
area = 3.1415 * radius * radius;
```

This line is an assignment statement that multiplies the number `3.1415` with the value stored in the variable `radius`, then multiplies the product by the value stored in `radius` again. The result is stored in the variable named `area`.

Finally, to output the results to the user, the `printf()` function is used like this:

```
printf("The Area is %f\n", area);
```

This line calls the `printf()` function again. However, this call is a little different. Notice that two parameters are passed to the function and that the funny `%f` character is showing up again.

The `%f` is used here as it was in the `scanf()` function, with one exception. Rather than inputting a floating-point number from the user, you use this character to display a number as a floating-point value on-screen. The number you want to display is stored in the variable named `area` and, coincidentally, `area` shows up as the last parameter to the function.

The `\n` after the `%f` characters is an *escape character.* It sends a carriage return and line-feed combination to the screen. The escape character causes your program to move the cursor to the next line on-screen.

Returning to Cloud Nine

The last statement before the closing curly brace inside the program is

```
return 0;
```

The `return` statement exits the current function. In this case, the statement returns the program to the operating system, then passes a return value to the operating system. When exiting from the `main()` function, the return value denotes an error value. Listing 2.1 returns 0, denoting that no error occurred.

Listing 2.1 initially defined `main()` so it would return only an integer value (remember the declaration, `int main()`, at the beginning of the program?). The error code value can be checked by a batch file that can, in turn, cause different programs to be executed.

The ANSI definition of the language requires that the `main()` function return an integer value. In practice, the return value is not used much. In fact, if you turn ANSI compatibility off, most compilers enable you to declare `main()` to return no value.

Learning More About C

Turbo C++ comes with an extensive set of built-in library functions that help you write your programs. The `printf()` and `scanf()` functions are just two of these library functions. Because the compiler provides a number of ready-to-run library functions, you can use the compiler more quickly than if you had to write your own functions.

It is important to note that these library functions don't compose the standard definition of the language. Because these functions aren't mandatory, the compiler company has the freedom to decide which library functions to include in the language.

Notice that every line of the program inside the braces is terminated with a semicolon (;). In C, statements are separated with the semicolon. It is this semicolon that separates one line from the next on the screen.

The C programming language does not recognize "whitespace" characters—carriage returns, tabs, and spaces. You can put as many whitespace characters in your program as you like. It does not matter to the C compiler (except within a literal string). In fact, the whitespace characters are invisible to the compiler.

> **NOTE** Whitespace characters are recognized by C only within a literal string. Because whitespace is not recognized anywhere else, use it liberally in your program to improve readability.

Listing 2.1, FIRST.C, would compile and run exactly the same if you had entered it in the following format:

```
int main()
{
  float area, radius;printf("Please Enter Radius: ");
  scanf("%f", &radius);area = PI * radius * radius;
  printf("The Area is %f\n", area);return 0;
     }
```

Similarly, the program would run the same if it had the following format:

```
int main(){float area,
     radius;printf("Please Enter Radius: ");
scanf("%f", &radius);area = PI * radius * radius;
     printf("The Area is %f\n", area);return 0;}
```

Although the two preceding examples are treated the same by the compiler, the code obviously looks different to users and programmers. The second example makes the program structure difficult to spot. The first appearance of the program (in Listing 2.1) is the easiest method for humans to understand.

Because the compiler is so flexible, C programmers are able to use their own programming styles. All programs conform to a similar style throughout this book. The most important style point to adopt is the alignment of matching braces. This procedure makes it easier to ensure that every opening brace has a closing brace. Also, the program is usually spaced so it's easier to understand.

Summary

This chapter examined the basic structure of a typical C program. You learned about preprocessor directives, program variables, C statements, and the main entry point of a C program.

In particular, you learned the following topics:

- Elements of a C program include *preprocessor directives, variable declarations, function declarations,* and the *`main()` function.* The `main()` function receives control when the program begins to run. There can be only *one* `main()` function in every program.

- The C programming language is *case-sensitive.* That is, it treats upper- and lowercase letters separately. The identifiers LANGUAGE, Language, languagE, and LaNgUaGe are each unique to a C program.

- *Comments* are used in a C program to help humans understand exactly what is happening in the code. Comments are ignored by the compiler. They begin with the `/*` characters and end with the `*/` characters.

- *Preprocessor directives* begin with a pound sign (#) and give instructions to the C preprocessor. They are carried out before the compiler compiles the code. The `#include` preprocessor directive is used to include a file in another file. The included file is usually called a *header file.*

- *Curly braces* signal a block of code. The opening brace ({) signifies the beginning of a block of code. The closing brace (}) terminates a block of code.

- Every statement in a C program is terminated with a semicolon (;) character. Whitespace characters (carriage returns, tabs, and spaces) are not recognized by the C programming language as terminators.

CHAPTER THREE

Variables and Operators

A C program consists of variables, functions, and operators. These are the fundamental parts of any computer language. A *variable* is a symbolic name that can be assigned different values. A *function* is a section of code that performs a particular operation (discussed in Chapter 7). *Operators* are words or symbols that cause a program to take action on a variable.

A variable is stored in the computer's memory. When a variable receives a value, that value is placed in the memory space designated for the symbol corresponding to that variable. Different types of variables require different amounts of memory storage. As with most computer languages, C supports several different types of variables. Unlike other computer languages, however, C allows great versatility in declaring variable types. The first part of this chapter explains C variables and data types.

The C programming language includes a large number of operators that fall into several different categories. The second half of this chapter examines the most common operators. Specifically, you will see how assignment operators, arithmetic operators, relational tests, and logical operators are used to form expressions.

Using Variables

All variables in C must be declared prior to use. Pascal is another language that has this requirement. It is necessary because the compiler must know what type of data a variable holds before it can properly compile other statements that rely on the variable. This process is part of what makes a C compiler efficient when compared to languages such as BASIC.

A *data type* is a set of values that represents a particular variable in memory. The C programming language has four basic data types, as listed:

- integer (`int`)
- floating point (`float`)
- double precision (`double`)
- character (`char`)

When declaring your variables, you must consider what the variables will hold and declare them based on this information. The data type of a variable determines what type of data the variable can contain, as well as the range of values the variable can store.

Syntax at a Glance

Variable Declarations

The general form of a variable declaration statement is as follows:

```
VariableType VariableNameList;
```

Here, `VariableType` is a valid C data type, and *`VariableNameList`* is one or more identifier names separated with commas.

Examples of variable declarations follow:

```
float total;
int x, y;
double a, b, radius;
char ch;
```

The first declaration defines a variable, `total`, to be of type `float` (floating point). The second declaration creates two integer variables named `x` and `y`. In C, it is legal to declare multiple variables on one line. Such a declaration saves space and typing time. The third declaration creates three variables of type `double`. The last declaration creates a variable named `ch` of type `char` (character).

> **Variable Declarations**
> A variable name can consist of letters and digits. However, the first character must be a letter. Both upper- and lowercase identifiers are permitted. The underscore character (_) can be used also in a variable declaration. An underscore is often used in the middle of an identifier, to make the identifier easier to read (for example, `database_identifier` and `create_icon_indirect`).

In the following sections, you learn the types of variables that C provides. You also learn the difference between constants and variables.

Using Integer Variables

Integers consist of any valid combination of digits along with a plus or minus sign. An *integer* is a number that does not contain a decimal point. Integers in mathematics are whole numbers and can be negative or positive. Examples of integers include:

```
1676, -49, 0, 61841, -123
```

Notice that integers can be positive or negative. If a plus sign (+) is not declared, the variable is assumed to be positive. To declare a number negative, it must include the (–) symbol. The number 0 (zero) is also included in the set of integers.

Example integer variable declarations include:

```
int counter;
int x, y, center, radius;
int bikes = 12;
```

To declare an integer, you first list the reserved word `int` and then list the names of the variables to declare. The keyword `int` signals your program to set aside enough space for the integer and to assign the name following the keyword to represent that memory space.

The third declaration in the previous code sets up a variable named `bikes` and assigns it an initial value. Assigning an initial value to a variable is often very useful. You cannot assume that a variable is assigned any specific value when you first declare it. If you want it to be a certain value, you must do it yourself.

CAUTION

Using an uninitialized variable can have unpredictable results. You should never rely on a variable having a specific value, unless you implicitly assign the variable a value.

Listing 3.1 declares an integer variable and gives it a value. When you execute the program, it creates the variable and assigns it an integer value. Also, the value of the integer is displayed on-screen.

Listing 3.1. Using an integer-number variable.

```
/************************************************
  INT.C - Uses an integer number.
  Crash Course in C by Paul J. Perry
 ************************************************/

#include <stdio.h>

int main()
{
   int x;

   x = 456;
   printf("The value of x is %d\n", x);

   return 0;
}
```

Notice the use of the assignment statement, which assigns the value of 456 to the variable `x`. The `=` is the assignment operator—it gives the variable on the left side the value of the constant on the right side.

There are three types of integers in C. They are: `int`, `short`, and `long`. The `int` type provides the most common integer type used. The `short` type is the same as an `int` on all PC-based C compilers (two bytes). A `long` integer type is four bytes. A `long` variable can therefore hold a much larger value. The three types of integers provide a means of specifying a more exact size or range of values the variables can hold.

Every `int` variable requires two bytes of memory and holds numbers in the range –32,768 to 32,767. You will see how this compares to the memory requirements of other variable types as you read about them in this chapter. You will find that two bytes is a rather small amount of memory. For this reason, integers are commonly used as counters in program loops and temporary variables.

Using Floating-Point Variables

Floating-point variables are used when your program uses fractional components or when your application requires extremely large or small numbers. Floating-point variables represent numbers with a decimal place. Examples include:

```
3.1415927, .00001676, and 49.678
```


There are three basic types of floating-point numbers: `float`, `double`, and `long double`. The difference between them is the magnitude of the largest, as well as the smallest, number they can hold. First take a look at type `float`, the smallest of the floating-point variable types.

Type *float*

Variables defined as `float` can be in the range $3.4x10^{+38}$ to $3.4x10^{-38}$ and occupy four bytes of memory. Precision is set to seven digits of accuracy.

Floating-point variables require more memory to be stored. As a result, the computer takes longer to process information with a variable declared as a `float` or a `double`.

Choosing the correct data type is an important aspect of creating optimized programs that run quickly and efficiently. The following examples show several floating-point variable declarations:

```
float diameter;
float principal, interest;
float distance = 25.05;
```

The first declaration is the simplest. It declares a single variable with no initial value. The second declaration shows how to declare multiple variables on a single line. The third declaration shows the assignment of an initial value to the variable.

Listing 3.2 shows how to use floating-point variables in a program. It prompts the user to enter three weights, then calculates the average weight.

Listing 3.2. A program that calculates the average of three weights.

```
/**************************************************
  FLOAT.C - Example of using floating-point numbers.
  Crash Course in C by Paul J. Perry
 *************************************************/

#include <stdio.h>

int main()
{
   float avg;
   float weight1, weight2, weight3;

   printf("Enter first person's weight\n");
   scanf("%f", &weight1);

   printf("Enter second person's weight\n");
   scanf("%f", &weight2);

   printf("Enter third person's weight\n");
   scanf("%f", &weight3);

   avg = (weight1 + weight2 + weight3) / 3;

   printf("Average weight is %f\n", avg);

   return 0;
}
```

A sample interaction with Listing 3.2 looks like:

```
Enter first person's weight
145
Enter second person's weight
167
Enter third person's weight
130
Average weight is 147.333328
```

You can see how the program inputs the three values and then calculates the average value, depending on which numbers the user enters. Anybody with programming experience would laugh at the efficiency of this program because the groups of `printf()` and `scanf()` functions can be easily executed several times in a loop. The loop would save repetitive code. Loops, however, aren't covered until Chapter 6. For now, just know that they can be done.

Type *double*

The second type of floating-point value is `double`. Variables of type `double` require eight bytes of memory to be stored and can hold numbers in the range $1.7x10^{-308}$ to $1.7x10^{+308}$. The larger size gives better precision and range, but also uses more memory. Because they can hold larger values, numbers of type `double` are often used in scientific and financial calculations.

Examples of `double` variable declarations follow:

```
double value;
double pi = 3.2425927;
```

The first line creates a `double` variable with the name `value`. The second creates a `double` variable with the name `pi` and assigns it an initial value.

Type *long double*

A `long double` requires 10 bytes of memory and can store values in the range $3.4x10^{-4932}$ to $3.4x10^{+4932}$. A `long double` requires 10 bytes of memory. The size of the numbers it can hold depends on the type of compiler you are using. Some example declarations include:

```
long double very_big_number;
long double variable1, variable2;
```

Notice that this variable type requires two keywords. The `long` keyword is actually a type modifier that modifies the basic definition of the `double` type. Besides providing a greater array of values to be stored, a `long double` provides more precise values. A `long double` has 19 digits of precision.

Using Character Variables

Most variable types are numeric, but there is one that isn't. It is the character (`char`) type. A character is a single letter surrounded by single quotations (actually apostrophes). Character variables are used to hold eight-bit ASCII characters, such as `'A'`, `'P'`, `'1'` or any other eight-bit quantity. A character variable uses one byte in memory.

Character variables are used to represent the ASCII character set. An ASCII code is actually just a number used to represent a symbol. Sometimes, you will find that variables of type `char` and type `int` are similar and can be used interchangeably.

To declare two character variables, use the following statement:

```
char letter1, letter2;
```

You might want to assign special control codes to characters. For example, C defines certain codes used to assign a control code to a variable. Table 3.1 displays these special character constants.

NOTE The special character constants are useful when you have special formatting needs for the output of your program.

Table 3.1. Special character constants.

Code	*Description*
'\a'	Bell
'\\'	Backslash
'\b'	Backspace
'\r'	Carriage return
'\"'	Double quotations
'\f'	Form feed
'\n'	Newline character
'\0'	Null value
'\''	Single quotation
'\t'	Tab
'\v'	Vertical Tab

To assign a backslash character to a code, use the following line of code:

```
char ch = '\\'
```

The other special codes are used in a similar manner.

Using Constant Values

Constants are identifiers that cannot change during execution of your program. A program can have constants of any of the five basic data types. There are integer constants, floating-point constants, and character constants.

A constant is declared using the reserved word `const`, followed by the identifier, and then an assignment statement. Examples of constant declarations include:

```
const int speed = 75;
const float pi = 3.1415927;
const double diameter = 899.567;
const char ch = 'P';
```

Notice that the only difference between variable declarations and constant declarations is the reserved word `const`. All the constants are given a value that cannot change during the execution of a program. Remember that earlier, you could give a variable a beginning value, but that value could be changed during program execution.

Constants are similar to `#define` preprocessor directives that you learned about earlier. However, constants are easier to use while debugging. Constants are usually better to use than `#define` declarations. The reason that `#define` declarations are still around is because the original C language definition had no constant definition in the language. Therefore, programmers had no choice.

Constants cannot be changed during program execution. Listing 3.3 gives an example of using constants in the C programming language.

Listing 3.3. Sample constant program.

```
/**********************************************
  CONSTS.C - Sample program that uses constants.
  Crash Course in C by Paul J. Perry
 *********************************************/

#include <stdio.h>

int main()
{
   const char letter = 'X';
   const float pi = 3.1415927;
   const int value = 12345;

   printf("The constants include:\n\
     character      = %c\n\
       floating point = %f\n\
       integer        = %d\n",
       letter, pi, value);

   return 0;
}
```

CONST IS NOT DEFINED FOR NON ANSI C.
STATIC CHAR LETTER = 'X'; will compile

The first section of the program declares constant values. They are then displayed on the video screen.

> **NOTE** Notice the use of the ending backslash in the first four lines to the `printf()` function. This notation tells the compiler to combine physical lines into one. In this program, the first four lines of the `printf()` function call appear as a single line to the compiler.

A Variable Example

Take a look at an example of a program that uses different types of variables and constants. In Chapter 2, you saw how to declare and use a floating-point variable. The program in Listing 3.4 is an example that uses character, integer, and floating-point variables to get input from the user and display the user's value.

Listing 3.4. A program that uses a variety of variables.

```
/*************************************
  VARS.C - Program to show the use of
           variables in C.
  Crash Course in C by Paul J. Perry
*************************************/

#include <stdio.h>

int main()
{
   char letter;
   int number;
   float amount;
   const double pi = 3.14159;

   printf("Enter a Character\n");
   scanf("%c", &letter);

   printf("Enter an Integer Number\n");
   scanf("%d", &number);

   printf("Enter a Floating-Point Number\n");
```

```
    scanf("%f", &amount);

    printf("\n\n");

    printf("The character, 'letter' "
           "is equal to %c\n", letter);
    printf("The integer, 'number' "
           "is equal to %d\n", number);
    printf("The floating point, 'amount' "
            "is equal to %f\n", amount);
    printf("The double constant, 'pi' "
           "is equal to %f\n", pi);

    return 0;
}
```


The program uses the `printf()` and `scanf()` functions to display output and get input from the user. A sample interaction with the user looks like this:

```
Enter a Character
p
Enter an Integer Number
24
Enter a Floating-Point Number
768.867


The character, 'letter' is equal to p
The integer, 'number' is equal to 24
The floating point, 'amount' is equal to 768.867000
The double constant, 'pi' is equal to 3.141590
```

The first part of the program prompts the user to enter three types of variables. The user must press the Enter key each time in order for the computer to store the value in the computer.

The second part of the program displays the values of the three variables the user entered, along with the value of a floating-point constant declared at the beginning of the program.

Listing 3.4 is a simple example that shows how to use variables and constant values in your program. Throughout this book, you will see variables used—there is no getting away from them. A program without variables is like a sandwich without the meat.

Using Arrays

An *array* is a list (or table) of variables of a related type. The variables in an array have a common name. Each individual item in the array is accessed using an integer number called an *index*. Index values are always positive numbers.

Several rules exist when using and defining arrays, as follows:

- You must specify the *size* of the array, or how many elements it will hold.
- Arrays can also have two or more dimensions. Therefore, you also must specify the *number of dimensions* of the array.

The number of dimensions refers to how many index values are used to access variables in the array. A one-dimensional array has a single index value and is similar to a list of data. A two-dimensional array has two index values and can represent objects such as graph paper or spreadsheets with rows and columns. Figure 3.1 shows the concepts of both one-dimensional and two-dimensional arrays.

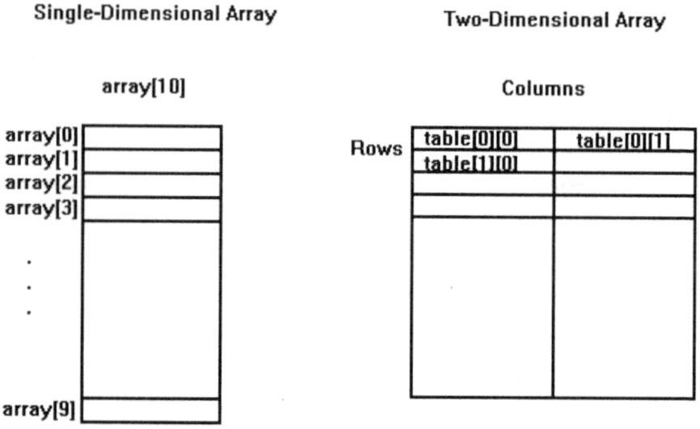

Figure 3.1. *Arrays: one- and two-dimensional.*

Single-Dimensional Arrays

The simplest type of array is the one-dimensional (or single-dimensional) array.

Syntax at a Glance

Arrays

The general form of a single-dimensional array is

```
datatype variablename[size];
```

whereby *datatype* declares the type of the array (`int`, `char`, `double`, and so on) of each element and *size* defines how many elements the array holds. The *variablename* is the identifier you give to the array.

For example, the following line declares an integer array named `table`, which is four elements in length:

```
int table[4];
```

To refer to the elements of the array, use the index value. All array elements are numbered starting at 0. Therefore, if you create an array with four elements, the first element is numbered 0, and the highest element is numbered 3. Here are the statements used to access the declared array elements:

```
table[0] = 1;
table[1] = 2;
table[2] = 3;
table[3] = 4;
```

The four variables, `table[0]`, `table[1]`, `table[2]`, and `table[3]` all share a common name. They are distinguished by means of the index value 0, 1, 2, or 3. Each of the four variables may be assigned a value. In the example above, the variables are assigned consecutive numbers from 1 to 4.

Bounds Checking

The C programming language performs no *bounds checking* on arrays. That is, there is no test to determine whether the index value used in an array exceeds the actual size of the array. Nothing stops you from accessing elements at the end of an array that were not previously declared. As the programmer, it is your job to ensure that all arrays are large enough to hold the data the program will put in them. If there is any reason to believe that your program may be accessing array elements outside of the declared array, you should add checks to the code to prevent it.

CAUTION

C does not stop you from accessing elements at the end of an array that were not previously declared. If this happens, you will be assigning values to some other variable's memory space. Data entered with too large a subscript will simply be placed in memory outside the array. This is something you have to be careful about.

You might be wondering why C does not provide bounds checking. The answer is that C was designed to compile programs that will execute as quickly as possible. Error checking slows the execution of a program. Therefore, it is the programmer's responsibility to prevent array overruns. Also, by not checking bounds, C gives the programmer more control over using variables in a program.

Initializing Arrays

Remember how you were able to declare a variable and initialize it to a specific value? You can do the same initialization trick with arrays. To initialize array elements to specific values, specify initialization values at the time you declare the array. Here is an example:

```
int numbers[5] = { 1, 135, 10, 71, 23 };
```

The list of values is enclosed in braces and the values are separated by commas.

Another form of array initialization enables you to omit the number that defines the size of the array. The compiler then counts the number of elements in the initialization list and creates an array with the appropriate size. For example:

```
int numbers[] = { 1, 135, 10, 71, 23 };
```

creates the same size array as above (with five elements), but it makes the compiler set the appropriate size of the array.

Multiple-Dimensional Arrays

The C programming language enables you to use multiple-dimensional arrays to reference more complex information.

The simplest form of the multiple-dimensional array is the two-dimensional array. You can think of a two-dimensional array as a list of one-dimensional arrays.

Two-dimensional arrays are defined in much the same manner as one-dimensional arrays, except that a separate pair of square brackets is required for each index. Thus, a two-dimensional array requires two pairs of square brackets. In general terms, a two-dimensional array is declared like so:

```
int twodim[5][10];
```

This declares a two-dimensional integer array named `twodim`. It can be thought of as a table having five rows and 10 columns.

The two-dimensional array declaration in C is a little different than in most computer languages. In Pascal, commas are usually used to separate array dimensions. However, C places each dimension in its own set of brackets. Be sure not to try to refer to a two-dimensional array element as `twodim[15,10]`. This will cause the compiler to issue an error message. Instead, the proper way to address this array element in C is `twodim[15][10]`.

Initializing Multiple-Dimensional Arrays

You learned how to initialize one-dimensional arrays earlier. Two-dimensional arrays can be initialized in a similar manner. For example, to initialize a two-dimensional array, use the following statement:

```
int initarr[3][5] =
   { { 45, 213, 78, 12, 98},
         { 12, 423, 27, 39, 76},
         { 19, 82,  47, 55, 100}  };
```

Again, as with single-dimensional arrays, the numbers in the brackets are optional. If they are not specified, the number of given elements is used as the size of the array.

String Variables

You might be wondering why you see a section about string variables mixed with arrays. The reason is that in C, there is no intrinsic string variable type. Instead, programmers make use of character arrays.

In C, a string is characterized as a number of character values terminated with a null value. A null is specified with the `'\0'` escape sequence. It looks like two characters, but is really one.

> **NOTE** Because of the null terminator, it is necessary to declare character arrays to be one character longer than the largest string they hold.

The general definition of a character array looks like this:

```
char string[size];
```

whereby *size* is the length of the string. Each character occupies one byte of memory. You must always make space for the terminating null character. Therefore, if you know a string will be 10 characters long, you must define it as 11 characters long when it is declared.

Initializing Strings

Just as numerical arrays can be initialized, so can character arrays. You can specify each character in the string, like this:

```
char name[] = { 'P', 'r', 'o', 'g', 'r', 'a',
                'm', 's', '\0'  };
```

However, you can alternatively specify the characters as a single string, using quotations, as follows:

```
char name[] = "Programs";
```

These two lines mean the same thing to the compiler. Notice that it is easier to type a full string than each character separated with apostrophes and commas. When declaring the entire string at once, you don't have to insert the terminating null character. The string initialization causes the null character to be added automatically.

An Array Example

The program in Listing 3.5 uses two arrays. It initializes an integer array with five values. It also uses a character array to store the name of the user. When the program is executed, it asks the user for her or his name. Once the user's name has been entered, the program displays a message with the name and the result of the average of the values inside the array.

THIS will NOT WORK WITH
NON ~~ANSI Compl~~ ANSI C compilers.

TRY:
CHAR *NAME = "PROGRAMS";

Listing 3.5. Program to demonstrate arrays in C.

```
/************************************
  ARRAY.C - Program to show the use of
            arrays in C.
  Crash Course in C by Paul J. Perry
 ************************************/

#include <stdio.h>

int main()
{
   int data[5] = { 10, 50, 100, 150, 200 };
   char name[80];
   long avg;

   avg = ( data[0] + data[1] + data[2] +
           data[3] + data[4] ) / 5;

   printf("Please Enter Your Name: ");
   scanf("%s", &name);

   printf("\n");          /* Carriage Return */

   printf("Hey %s, the average number is %d",
          name, avg);

   return 0;
}
```

When the program runs, it looks something like this:

```
Please Enter Your Name: Kevin

Hey Kevin, the average number is 102
```

Later, as you learn more about the C language, you will learn some ways to cycle through arrays that make them much easier.

For the rest of this chapter, turn your focus to another important part of C programming: operators.

Using Operators

Operators work so closely with variables that, just as it is hard to imagine a program without variables, it is difficult to create a useful C program that does not use operators. Remember that *operators* are words or symbols that cause a program to do something to its variables.

There are several different categories of operators. The rest of this section discusses how assignment operators, arithmetic operators, relational operators, unary operators, and logical operators are used to form expressions.

Assignment Operators

You have already seen the use of the assignment operator in Chapter 2. An example follows:

```
int num;
num = 11;
```

The first statement declares an integer variable. It is given an identifier (`num`) and a type (`int`). The second statement uses the assignment operator (=) to assign the variable a value. The assignment operator has the same function as the := operator in Pascal or the = operator in BASIC.

Assignment expressions that make use of the = operator are written in the form:

```
identifier = expression;
```

whereby *`identifier`* usually represents a variable and *`expression`* represents a constant, a variable, or a more complex expression.

Arithmetic Operators

You have already been introduced to arithmetic operators in Chapter 2 (there are some operators you cannot get around using when you try to teach the basics). The arithmetic operators enable you to perform basic mathematical operations. There are five arithmetic operators in C: addition, subtraction, multiplication, division, and remainder, as summarized in Table 3.2.

Table 3.2. Arithmetic operators in C.

Operator	*Purpose*
+	Addition
-	Subtraction
*	Multiplication
/	Division
%	Remainder (modulus operator)

The C programming language uses the four arithmetic operators that are common in most other programming languages, including BASIC and Pascal. It also uses one, the remainder operator, which is not as common.

The operands acted on by the arithmetic operators must represent numeric values. Thus, the operands can be integer, floating point, or characters (because characters variables are actually represented as integer quantities). Following the laws of mathematics, the division operator (/) requires that the second operand be nonzero.

Division of one integer value by another is referred to as integer division. The % operator is the remainder after dividing integer values. It is sometimes referred to as the *modulus operator*. It requires that both operands be integer variables as well as that the second operand be nonzero. The decimal portion of the quotient is always dropped in integer division.

The listing in Chapter 2 (FIRST.C) demonstrated the multiplication (*) operator. Remember that the listing included a statement, like this:

```
area = PI * radius * radius;
```

This statement multiplied the value of the variable radius by itself and then multiplied it by the value defined by PI. The result is assigned to the variable area.

Another example of multiplication is as follows:

```
days = age * 365;
```

Similar to the previous example, this one multiplies the value of the variable age (assumed to be in years) by the integer value 365 (the number of days in a year), thus informing the user how old they are in days. Both of the previous examples use simple multiplication.

Some more examples are

```
result = 365/5;
total = 27 + 83;
value = 99 - previous;
```

These are all basic mathematical equations that are easy to understand.

The C programming language can easily handle more complex expressions. As an exercise, you might try to write a program that combines the arithmetic operators to create more complex expressions.

Relational Operators

There are six relational operators in the C programming language. They are listed in Table 3.3.

Table 3.3. Relational operators in C.

Operator	*Explanation*	*Example(s)*	*Description*
<	Less than	5 < 10	5 is less than 10
>	Greater than	10 > 5	10 is greater than 5
==	Equal to	10 == 10	10 is equal to 10
!=	Not equal to	9 != 10	9 is not equal to 10
<=	Less than or equal to	5 <= 5	5 is less than or equal to 5
		5 <= 10	5 is less than or equal to 10
>=	Greater than or equal to	10 >= 10	10 is greater than or equal to 10
		20 >= 10	20 is greater than or equal to 10

Relational operators compare two values. If the values compare correctly according to the relational operator, the expression is considered true, otherwise it is considered false. The resulting expressions represent an expression of type integer, because true is represented by the integer value 1 and false is represented by the integer value 0.

For example, the expression `10 > 9` (10 is greater than 9) results in a true value. However, the expression `9 > 10` (9 is greater than 10) is a false expression. Listing 3.6 provides an example of the relational operators.

Listing 3.6. Working with relational operators.

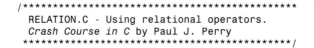

```
/*********************************************
  RELATION.C - Using relational operators.
  Crash Course in C by Paul J. Perry
*********************************************/
```

```
#include <stdio.h>

int main()
{
   int i;

   i = 9;

   printf("i is equal to %d\n\n",i);

   printf("i < 5 is %d\n",   i <  5);   /* False */
   printf("i > 4 is %d\n",   i >  4);   /* True  */
   printf("i == 9 is %d\n",  i == 9);   /* True  */
   printf("i != 8 is %d\n",  i != 8);   /* True  */
   printf("i <= 7 is %d\n",  i <= 7);   /* False */
   printf("i >= 6 is %d\n",  i >= 6);   /* True  */

   return 0;
}
```

The program declares a variable and assigns it a starting value. A series of relational tests is then carried out. The output of the program looks similar to this:

```
i is equal to 9

i < 5 is 0
i > 4 is 1
i == 9 is 1
i != 8 is 1
i <= 7 is 0
i >= 6 is 1
```

Each `printf()` statement includes a relational operator. It returns a value of 1 (true) or 0 (false). The tests in the sample program mimic the relational operators that are available.

Unary Operators

The C programming language includes some rather unique unary operators. Although only two of C's unary operators are covered here, they are the most interesting ones. The unary operators act on a single operand to produce a new value.

The two unary operators you are to learn are called the *increment operator* (++) , and the *decrement operator* (--). The increment operator increases its operand by one, whereas the decrement operator decreases its operand by one. These two operators work only on a single operand.

An example follows:

```
int i;
i = 0;
++i;
--i;
```

This example causes the integer variable `i` to be incremented by one (in the third line) and decremented by one (in the fourth line). This code is equal to the statements:

```
int i;
i = 0;
i = i + 1;
i = i - 1;
```

The increment and decrement operators are used in different ways, depending on whether the operator is written before or after the operand. If the operator precedes the operand (`++i`), the operand will be altered in value before it is used in the statement (this is called the *prefix operator*). If the operator follows the operand (`i++`), the value of the operand will be changed after the variable is used (this is called the *postfix operator*).

At this point, it may not seem important as to whether the operand is altered before or after it is used. Listing 3.7 gives a demonstration of the increment operator with both prefix and postfix notation. It should clear things up for you. Type and run the program now.

Listing 3.7. Decrement operator example.

```
/**************************************************
  UNARY.C - Shows the use of the decrement operator.
  Crash Course in C by Paul J. Perry
 **************************************************/

#include <stdio.h>

int main()
{
   int value;

   value = 10;

   printf("value = %d\n", value);
   printf("value = %d\n", --value);
   printf("value = %d\n", value);
   printf("value = %d\n", value--);
   printf("value = %d\n", value);

   return 0;
}
```

The program's output looks like this:

```
value = 10
value = 9
value = 9
value = 9
value = 8
```

The program declares an integer variable and assigns it a value of 10. The starting value of the variable is displayed in the first `printf()` statement. The next statement decrements the value of the variable and displays its output. It uses the prefix increment operator. The next line displays the new value of the variable (the same value as the one displayed in the previous line).

Now use the postfix version of the increment operator. Notice that the printed output for the fourth line is the same as the previous line. However, you know the variable was decremented, because when the final value is displayed, it is what you expect. This is due to the use of the postfix version of the increment operator.

This example illustrates the power of the decrement (and indirectly the increment) operator. These operators enable the programmer to have complete control of when the operator modifies the value and what value a program returns.

The increment and decrement unary operators are examples of operators in the C programming language that other programming languages just don't have. As you continue your search of C, you will discover more features of the language not available in other programming languages.

Logical Operators

In addition to the relational and equality operators, C contains three logical operators. They are presented in Table 3.4.

Table 3.4. Logical operators in C.

Operator	*Description*	*Explanation*
`&&`	AND	Result is true if both expressions are true.
`¦¦`	OR	Result is true if either expression is true.
`!`	NOT	Reverses the condition of the expression.

The logical operators are rather unique because they usually work on operands that also are logical expressions (although not always). The result of using logical operators on logical expressions is that simple statements are combined to create complex conditions.

To put this in the context of every day living, you would call an expression such as "If it is sunny, I will go swimming" a simple expression. Another simple expression might be "If I have time, I will go swimming". You can combine these two simple statements and say "If I have time AND if it is sunny, I will go swimming". This result is a complex statement.

Before looking at complex statements, get an overall feel for the use of logical operators.

The logical `AND` and logical `OR` operators work on two operands to return a logical value based on the operands. The logical `NOT` operator works on a single operand. Tables 3.5, 3.6, and 3.7 serve to show the results of the logical tests. Notice that every logical value is represented by either an *x* or *y* value. The result signifies how the logical operator is evaluated.

Table 3.5. Logical *AND (&&)* truth table.

x	*y*	*Result*
1	1	1 (true)
1	0	0 (false)
0	1	0 (false)
0	0	0 (false)

Table 3.6. Logical *OR (||)* truth table.

x	*y*	*Result*
1	1	1 (true)
1	0	1 (true)
0	1	1 (true)
0	0	0 (false)

Table 3.7. Logical *NOT (!)* truth table.

x	*Result*
1	0 (false)
0	1 (true)

To explain logical operators, several examples follow:

```
1 && 1
0 || 0
!1
```

The first statement is an example of the AND operator. If you look in the truth table, it should return a value of 1. This is the only time that the AND logical operator returns a true value. All other times it returns false.

The second statement shows the use of the OR operator. It returns a false condition. This is the one condition that the OR operator returns false. In all other cases in the table, it returns true.

The last statement demonstrates the NOT operator. It only takes one operator, and returns a logical expression that is the opposite of the one on which it operates.

Logical expressions are important to the way computers are used. Internally, the microprocessor uses logical tests only. Luckily, you do not always have to use them. However, C provides them to enable you to have close interaction with the internals of the microprocessor.

Listing 3.8 is an example of a program that uses complex logical statements. Type and execute the program now.

Listing 3.8. Example of complex logical statements.

```
/******************************************
  LOGIC.C - Tests the logical operators.
  Crash Course in C by Paul J. Perry
 ******************************************/

#include <stdio.h>

int main()
```

continues

Listing 3.8. Continued

```
{
   int a,b;

   a = 1;
   b = 2;

   printf("Beginning values:\n");
   printf("a = %d\nb = %d\n\n", a,b);
   printf("Tests:\n");
   printf("a == 1 is %d\n", a == 1);     /* True */
   printf("b != 1 is %d\n", b != 1);     /* True */
   printf("Therefore, (a == 1) "
          "&& (b != 1) is %d\n",
          "( a == 1 ) && ( b != 1 ) );

   return 0;
}
```

The program's output looks like this:

```
Beginning values:
a = 1
b = 2

Tests:
a == 1 is 1
b != 1 is 1
Therefore, (a == 1) && (b != 1) is 1
```

The program starts by assigning two variables (a and b) beginning values. It then displays the result of two simple statements. Finally, it combines the simple statements into a complex one and shows the result.

Understanding Operator Precedence

When you were working with arithmetic operators, you used parentheses to force the compiler to evaluate things in a different order. It is appropriate, then, to ask "How does the compiler evaluate operators?"

You must determine the order in which operators are applied. This is specified by *operator precedence.* Table 3.8 summarizes operator precedence. Operators with highest precedence (or those that are applied first) are at the top of the list and those with lower precedence are listed lower in the list.

Table 3.8. Operator precedence in C.

Operator Type	*Operators*	*Associativity*
Unary	`--`, `++`	Right to Left
Logical `NOT`	`!`	Right to Left
Multiplication	`*`, `/`, `%`	Left to Right
Addition	`+`, `-`	Left to Right
Relational	`<`, `<=`, `>`, `>=`	Left to Right
Relational (Equality)	`==`, `!=`	Left to Right
Logical `AND`	`&&`	Left to Right
Logical `OR`	¦¦	Left to Right
Assignment	`=`	Right to Left

Each group of operators in the table has a certain associativity. The operators are either evaluated from left or from right. The only time this table is used is when you mix operators of different types.

NOTE Remember that you can override the precedence of any of the operators with the use of parentheses.

Summary

This chapter delved into the heart of C programming. You examined the basic C data types, learned about arrays, and learned what operators are and which ones are available in C.

In particular, the following topics were covered in this chapter:

- A *variable* is the name for a location in memory. When a programmer declares a variable, the variable must be given a name (or identifier) and a type. The name determines how you refer to the variable. The type of the variable refers to how much memory you set aside for the variable and the size of the information the variable can hold.
- The C programming language has four basic *data types:* integer (`int`), floating point (`float`), double precision (`double`), and character (`char`).

- There are three basic types of *floating-point numbers:* `float`, `double` and `long double`. The difference among them is the magnitude of the largest and smallest number they can hold.
- *Constants* are identifiers that cannot be changed during program execution.
- *Arrays* are groups of similar or related variables that share a common name. Each element in an array is accessed using an index to the array. Arrays always start at index zero and go to one less than the length of the array.
- The C programming language performs no *bounds checking* on arrays. That is, there is no test to determine whether the index value used in an array exceeds the actual size of the array. Nothing stops you from accessing elements at the end of an array that were not declared. It is the programmer's responsibility to make sure that the subscripts of an array do not go beyond the size of the array.
- In C, *string variables* are actually arrays of characters. The string must be terminated with a `'\0'` escape character (null) to signify the end of the string.
- *Operators* are symbols that cause a program to do something to its variables.
- The *assignment operator* is used to assign the value of one identifier to another.
- The *arithmetic operators* in C include `+` (addition), `-` (subtraction), `*` (multiplication), `/` (division), and `%` (remainder).
- *Relational operators* compare two different values. If the values compare correctly according to the relational operator, the expression is considered true (1), otherwise the expression is considered false (0).
- *Unary operators* are unique to C and allow a variable to be incremented or decremented by one.
- *Logical operators* work on two operands to return a logical value based on the operands. The C language includes the `&&` (`AND`), `||` (`OR`), and `!` (`NOT`) logical operators.
- *Operator precedence* determines the order in which expressions are evaluated in C. Operators with the highest precedence are applied first. The order of precedence is listed in Table 3.8.

CHAPTER FOUR

Keyboard Input and Video Output

C does not directly provide for input and output operations. Instead, input and output are accomplished through the use of *library functions* (functions that come standard with the compiler). Most C compilers define a complete set of input and output functions that handle I/O operations.

An I/O function is accessed from anywhere in a program by writing the function name, followed by a list of arguments in parentheses. The arguments represent data items that are sent to the function. Some I/O functions do not require arguments, but empty parentheses must still appear in the function call.

To access the input/output functions, your compiler usually provides a collection of header files. These files contain the necessary information to support the various types of I/O functions. As a rule, the header file required by the standard group of input/output library functions is STDIO.H. It is used in all programs that interact with the user.

Buffered I/O

The C input and output functions use a type of *buffered* input. Buffered input is the result of collecting and storing the characters you typed in an area of temporary memory called a *buffer*. When you are done entering the text, you press the Enter key, causing the block of characters to become available to the input routine. The characters are not sent to the input routine (and therefore, not available to your program) until you press Enter.

A program that immediately echoes input characters uses a form of *unbuffered* input. This means that the characters entered by the user are *immediately* available to your program. For example, if typing the letter *A* causes an action to immediately take place, you have witnessed unbuffered input. If, on the other hand, you type the letter *A*, then must press the Enter key to force the input to be accepted, you are using a form of buffered input.

There are several advantages of buffered input. First, if you incorrectly type something, you can use the Backspace key to correct your mistake. When you finally press the Enter key, your program receives the corrected version of the input. Furthermore, it is less time consuming to transmit characters as a single block than to send them one at a time.

Unbuffered input is desirable for real-time or interactive applications. For example, if you were writing a fast-paced, action packed arcade game you would not want to force the user to press the Enter key every time keyboard input is expected. In a spreadsheet program, as another example, each command should execute as soon as the user presses a key for best user-program interaction. For example, the user should be able to press F9 to have the spreadsheet calculated, rather than having to press F9 and Enter.

Thus, both buffered and unbuffered input have their places. You might wonder which type of buffering to use in your program. As the examples illustrate, it usually depends on what type of program you are writing. Also, it depends on the type of system on which you are running your program.

NOTE The ANSI C specification does not include functions for unbuffered keyboard input. However, most C compilers have extended the standard runtime library to include unbuffered input.

Character I/O

You can input single characters with the C library function `getchar()`. The `getchar()` function is a part of the standard group of I/O library routines. Therefore, the compiler requires the use of the STDIO.H header file for prototype information. The `getchar()` function returns a single character from the standard input device (usually the keyboard). The function does not require any arguments, although a pair of empty parentheses must follow the function name.

Syntax at a Glance

Buffered Character I/O

In general, the `getchar()` function is written as follows:

```
character_variable = getchar();
```

whereby *`character_variable`* refers to some previously declared character variable—defined by the programmer before using the variable. Note that `getchar()` reads from the standard input device and is also buffered; this means it does not return a value until you press Enter—see below:

```
char c;       /* declare variable */
c = getch(); /* get character value */
```

The counterpart to the `getchar()` function is the `putchar()` function. It displays a single character on the video display. The `putchar()` function is part of the standard C language I/O library. It outputs a single character to the standard output device (the video display). The character to be displayed is represented as a character type variable. The character is expressed as an argument to the function, enclosed in parentheses. In general, a reference to the `putchar()` function is as follows:

```
putchar(character_variable);
```

whereby *`character_variable`* refers to some previously declared character variable. The following code shows how `putchar()` is used:

```
char c = 'X'; /* declare variable */
putchar(c);   /* display variable */
```


Listing 4.1 shows how to use the `getchar()` and `putchar()` functions. It waits for you to enter a keypress. It then displays that keypress on-screen.

Listing 4.1. Character I/O example.

```
/**************************************************
  CHARIO.C - Inputing and outputing a character
             variable.
  Crash Course in C by Paul J. Perry
**************************************************/
```

continues

Listing 4.1. Continued

```
#include <stdio.h>

int main()
{
   char c;

   c = getchar();
   putchar(c);

   return 0;
}
```

Notice the use of the STDIO.H header file included at the beginning of the program. This .H file defines standard input and output for the C language (it is required in almost every program). As your programs become longer, it is not uncommon to include a long list of header files at the beginning.

Unbuffered Character I/O

Both the Borland and Microsoft compilers on the PC have unbuffered character I/O routines. The `getch()` function reads a character from the keyboard without any buffering. Furthermore, the character that the user entered is not displayed on-screen.

To get unbuffered input from the keyboard and display it on-screen at the same time, use the `getche()` function (the *e* stands for echo).

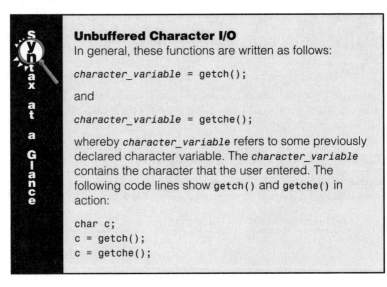

Syntax at a Glance

Unbuffered Character I/O

In general, these functions are written as follows:

```
character_variable = getch();
```

and

```
character_variable = getche();
```

whereby *`character_variable`* refers to some previously declared character variable. The *`character_variable`* contains the character that the user entered. The following code lines show `getch()` and `getche()` in action:

```
char c;
c = getch();
c = getche();
```

Unbuffered Character I/O
These two functions don't buffer their input. In other words, the function returns immediately when the user presses the appropriate key. The only difference between `getch()` and `getche()` is that `getche()` echoes the character to the video display (hence, the *e* in its name), whereas `getch()` does not.

Formatted I/O

Before you can start using the formatted keyboard and screen I/O functions, you have to know how C handles input, output, and data. C uses *streams* to represent the data that moves in and out of a program. C streams enable you to use your computer's I/O devices without worrying about low-level control of your computer. It is through streams that you do most types of I/O with the system. In Chapter 11, "Working with Files," you learn how disk files are accessed through streams.

Streams are a portable way to handle input/output tasks. They are used for all types of input and output, including manipulation of data files. The powerful aspect of using streams with C is that the code is transferable to different compilers on different computer platforms.

This might not seem powerful if you write programs for only one computer system, but large system houses use C entirely for this one benefit. When one wants to write a program for a different computer, one can simply transfer the C code to the new system and make small changes. If you had to rewrite the program for each platform, it would take much more time and energy.

Most C compilers provide several predefined streams for use in your programs. Whenever you write a C program, you automatically have access to the following standard streams:

Stream Name	*Description*	*Device*
stdin	Input Stream	Keyboard
stdout	Output Stream	Video Display
stdprn	Printer Stream	Printer Port
stdaux	Auxiliary Output	Serial Port
stderr	Error Stream	Video Display

Using these standard streams is easy because you do not have to do any extra housekeeping chores (such as is required when accessing disk files). C automatically opens the standard streams so they are available when your program is executing.

Formatted I/O Functions

You have briefly been exposed to the two basic methods of formatted I/O functions in Chapter 1: the `scanf()` and `printf()` functions. *Formatted input and output* refers to the capability to input data from the user in a format with which you are familiar. For example, you are familiar with the floating-point number, 3.1415. You are not familiar with the binary codes that store the number in memory. Formatted I/O is basically an easier way for the programmer to access data.

The `printf()` and `scanf()` functions both work with formatted data. The `scanf()` function gets input from the user, whereas the `printf()` function displays output to the user. When using either function, specify the type of data with which you are working.

Both `printf()` and `scanf()` work with C's basic data types. For example, you can use these functions to input integer data just as easily as you can use them to input floating-point data or character data.

The *printf()* Function

The `printf()` function consists of two main parts: a format string and a variable argument list. The format string specifies what type of data is output. The variable argument list supplies that data. Table 4.1 is a list of valid format specifiers for the `printf()` function.

Table 4.1. Format specifiers for the *printf()* function.

Format Specifier	*Output Type*
`%d`	Signed decimal integer
`%f`	Floating point
`%e`	Floating point with exponential notation

Format Specifier	*Output Type*
%x	Unsigned hexadecimal integer
%o	Unsigned octal integer
%c	Character
%s	String

Syntax at a Glance

Output with *printf()*

In general terms, the `printf()` function is accessed as follows:

```
printf("control string", arg1, arg2, ..., argx);
```

whereby *`control string`* refers to a string that contains formatting information, and *`arg1, arg2, ..., argx`* are arguments that represent the individual output data items. The arguments can be written as constants, single variable names, or more complex expressions.

The control string comprises individual groups of characters, with one character group for each output data item. Each character group must begin with the percent sign (%). The combination of a character group with the percent sign is known as a *format specifier.* The following code shows how to output text with `printf()`:

```
int x = 999;
printf("Now is the time");
printf("An integer is %d", 123);
printf("An integer variable is %d", x);
```

The first line displays the entire string passed to it on the video display. The second line displays an integer constant and the third line displays an integer variable.

The simplest form of the `printf()` function is one without the variable argument list. The variable argument list for the `printf()` function is not required. It is perfectly legal to use the function without specifying the argument list. For example:

```
printf("This will be displayed on the screen\n");
```

This line of code simply uses the `printf()` function to print a message on-screen.

CAUTION

If you use format specifiers, you must make sure that the conversion specifications match the variables you provide. A mismatch between the format string and the variable argument list causes strange program behavior.

An example line of code that uses a format specifier follows:

```
printf("The value is %d", result);
```

When the compiler interprets this line, it replaces the value of the variable `result` with the format specifier. For example, if the value of the variable `result` is equal to five, the output would look like this:

```
The value is 5
```

The compiler automatically replaces the `%d` with the value of `result`.

You can insert many special escape codes in a control string to control output. These codes enable you to output characters that do not appear on the keys of your keyboard. Table 4.2 lists the special escape codes that you can use in a string.

Table 4.2. Special escape sequences.

Code	*Description*
`\\`	Backslash
`\b`	Backspace
`\r`	Carriage return
`\"`	Double quotations
`\f`	Formfeed
`\n`	Newline
`\0`	Null value
`\'`	Single quotation
`\t`	Tab
`\v`	Vertical Tab

Code	*Description*
`\a`	Bell
`\ooo`	ASCII character in octal
`\x###`	Hex character
`\?`	Question mark

The most frequently used control sequence is the `\n` or newline escape sequence. It separates lines of output. In the following code fragment, it is used to separate output lines between subsequent `printf()` calls.

```
printf("One\nTwo\nThree");
```

This line appears on-screen as follows:

```
One
Two
Three
```

The `\n` code instructs the `printf()` function to separate the output lines by inserting a carriage return and line feed every time the `\n` code is located in the control string.

You can also pass values to the `printf()` function in hexadecimal. As you know, every character is represented in the computer by an ASCII (American Standard Code for Information and Interchange) value. You can use the `\xddd` escape sequence to specify a hex value to the `printf()` function. Listing 4.2 gives an example.

Listing 4.2. Displaying hex values with *printf()*.

```
/************************************************
  HEX.C - Displaying hex values.
  Crash Course in C by Paul J. Perry
 ************************************************/

#include <stdio.h>

int main()
{
   printf("\x048\x065\x06c\x06c\x06f\x020");
   printf("\x057\x06f\x072\x06c\x064\x021\n");
   printf("\n");
   return 0;
}
```

The output of Listing 4.2 looks like:

```
Hello World!
```

You would never guess the output by examining the code. The reason being that you specified each letter in the string `"Hello World!"` with its ASCII code in hex. You probably would not use this method of displaying characters very often. However, it does come in handy when you are trying to display some special characters.

Listing 4.3 shows another example of using the `printf()` function in a program. The program, PRINTF.C, requests the user to enter a number in inches. It then converts the value to centimeters and displays the result on-screen.

Listing 4.3. Inches-to-centimeters conversion program.

```
/*************************************************
  PRINTF.C - Sample program showing use of the
             printf() function.
  Crash Course in C by Paul J. Perry
 *************************************************/

#include <stdio.h>

int main()
{
   float inches, cent;
                 /* Variable declarations */

   printf("How many inches? ");
   scanf("%f", &inches);
                 /* Get input from user */
   cent = inches * 2.54;
                 /* Calculation */
   printf("%.2f Inches is %.2f Centimeters\n", inches, cent);

   return 0;
}
```

The following is a sample execution of the PRINTF.C program:

```
How many inches? 4.5
4.50 Inches is 11.43 Centimeters
```

The screen shows the conversion of 4.5 inches into 11.43 centimeters. The program uses the `scanf()` function to prompt the user for the number of inches (you will learn the `scanf()` function later in this chapter). It then does the calculation. Finally, the program uses the `printf()` function to demonstrate the use of the `%f` format specifier to display the values. The lines look a little different from what Table 4.2 shows because the lines use a field-width specifier to format the data:

```
printf("%.2f Inches is %.2f Centimeters\n", inches, cent);
```

The entered number, 4.5, was later displayed as 4.50. The `%.2f` format specifier instructs the `printf()` function to use the format specifier for floating-point numbers. A `.2` was placed between the `%` and the `f` in the previous example to further customize the output. This specification enables the programmer to control how many characters are printed following the decimal point. In this example, two characters are displayed. That is why the 4.5 was displayed as 4.50.

The programmer can also control how many spaces are printed before the decimal point. A digit preceding the decimal point determines the space created to hold the number when it is displayed. This is helpful in lining up tables of numbers with a decimal point. Here is a code example:

```
printf("%6.2f%6.2f%6.2f\n", 1.6, 49.01, 1600.2);
printf("%6.2f%6.2f%6.2f\n", 1600.2, 1.6, 49.01);
```

The following lines are the result of this function:

```
   1.60    49.01  1600.2
1600.20     1.6     49.01
```

Notice how the decimal points are aligned. Although the format specifiers may be confusing, the output is formatted nicely.

Next, take a look at the effect of the field-width modifiers on printing output. Study Listing 4.4.

Listing 4.4. Field-width specifiers example.

```
/********************************************
  WIDTHSP.C - Example of width specifiers.
  Crash Course in C by Paul J. Perry
********************************************/

#include <stdio.h>

int main()
{
   const int value = 768;

   printf("[%d]\n", value);
```

continues

Listing 4.4. Continued

```
    printf("[%2d]\n", value);
    printf("[%5d]\n", value);
    printf("[%10d]\n", value);

    return 0;
}
```

The program uses the brackets to show where each field begins and ends. The output of the program looks like:

```
[768]
[768]
[  768]
[       768]
```

The first conversion specification is `%d` with no width specifier. This specification produces a field with the default width as the size of the integer being printed. The second width specification is `%2d`. This produces a field width three digits long and the field is automatically expanded to fit the number.

The next conversion specification is `%5d`. This produces a field of five digits long. Notice that there are three spaces for the number and two additional blank spaces. The final specification `%10d` produces a field 10 spaces wide.

It is also possible to specify the maximum number of decimal places for a floating-point value, or the maximum number of characters for a string. This specification is known as the *field precision.* The precision is an unsigned integer that is preceded by a decimal place.

Sometimes a floating-point number is rounded if it must be shortened to conform to a precision specification. Take a look at Listing 4.5. This is a program that illustrates the use of the precision feature with floating-point numbers.

Listing 4.5. Example of precision specification with *printf()*.

```
/**************************************************
  PRECISE.C - Using precision with printf().
  Crash Course in C by Paul J. Perry
 **************************************************/


#include <stdio.h>
```

```
int main()
{
   float y = 123.456;

   printf("%7f %7.3f %7.1f\n", y, y, y);
   printf("%12e %12.5e %12.3e", y, y, y);

   return 0;
}
```

When the program is executed, the following output is generated:

```
123.456001 123.456   123.5
1.23456e+002 123456e+002   1.235e+002
```

The first line is produced by using the `%f` format specifier. Notice the rounding that occurs in the third value (`123.5`) because of the single decimal place precision specification. You can also see the leading blanks that were added as a result of the width specifier of seven characters.

The second line uses the `%e` format specifier. You can see the use of exponential notation used to display the value. Again, the third number is rounded to conform to the specified precision.

A minimum field width specification is not necessary with the precision specification. It is possible to specify the precision without the minimum field width, in which case the precision must still be preceded by a decimal point.

In summary, the format specifier in the `printf()` function determines the interpretation of a variable's type, the width of the field, the number of decimal places printed, and the justification.

The *scanf()* Function

You can enter data into the computer from a standard input device by means of the library function `scanf()`. You can use this function to enter any combination of numerical values and single characters. The function returns the number of data items that have been entered correctly.

Using the `scanf()` function to get data is an example of buffered input—the user must press Enter or Return after entering the data.

Syntax at a Glance

Input with *scanf()*

In general, the `scanf()` function has the following parameters:

```
scanf(control string, arg1, arg2, ..., argx);
```

whereby *`control string`* refers to a string containing certain required formatting information, and *`arg1, arg2, ..., argx`* are arguments that represent the individual data items. Actually, the arguments represent pointers that indicate the addresses of the data items in the computer's memory.

The control string comprises individual groups of characters, with one character group for each input data item. Each character group must begin with a percent sign (`%`). In its simplest form, a single character group consists of the percent sign, followed by a conversion character indicating the type of the corresponding data item.

The multiple-character groups in the control string can be adjacent, or they can be separated by whitespace characters (blank spaces, tabs, or carriage returns). If the control string contains any blanks or tabs, they are ignored.

If whitespace characters are used to separate multiple-character groups in the control string, all consecutive whitespace characters in the input data are read but ignored. The use of blank spaces as character group separators is common. Table 4.3 is a list of the `scanf()` conversion codes. The following code shows `scanf()` in action:

```
int x;
scanf("%d",&x);
```

CAUTION

Remember that `scanf()` parameters are pointers, whereas `printf()` parameters are real values, not pointers. Confusing these two can cause unexpected results—your program will probably compile, yet your system will probably crash!

Table 4.3. *scanf()* conversion codes.

Character	*Description*
`%c`	Single Character
`%d`	Signed decimal integer
`%e`	Floating-point value in exponential format
`%f`	Floating-point value
`%h`	Short integer
`%i`	Integer
`%o`	Octal integer
`%s`	String of characters
`%u`	Unsigned decimal integer
`%x`	Hexadecimal integer

Listing 4.6 is an example of the `scanf()` function in action.

Listing 4.6. Sample *scanf()* program.

```
/************************************************
  SCANF.C - Sample program showing use of scanf()
            function.
  Crash Course in C by Paul J. Perry
 ************************************************/

#include <stdio.h>

int main()
{
   float age, days;

   printf("How many years old are you? ");
   scanf("%f", &age);
   days = age * 365;
   printf("\nYou are %.1f days old.\n", days);

   return 0;
}
```

The program prompts the user for his or her age in years. It then converts the number of years to days by multiplying by 365 (the program does not check for leap years) and displaying the person's age in days. Program execution looks something like this:

```
How many years old are you? 55

You are 20075.0 days old.
```

As you can see, the format specifiers for the `scanf()` function look much like that for the `printf()` function. As with `printf()`, the first argument is a string that contains the format specifiers. In this case there is only one (`%f`). The following parameters are variable names. This program introduces a new symbol: the ampersand (`&`) added to the beginning of variable arguments.

> **NOTE** As mentioned earlier, the arguments to the `scanf()` function are actually the addresses of variables, rather than the actual variables. The `&` character returns the actual memory address of a variable. This is an important concept in C programming—you learn about it in more detail in Chapter 9.

Remember that you should use an ampersand (`&`) before the variable name when calling to `scanf()`. By far, the most common error is writing:

```
scanf("%d", i);
```

rather than

```
scanf("%d", &i);
```

The compiler does not generally detect this error, and no warning message is displayed. It causes your program to operate improperly and is usually a headache to track down.

By specifying an ampersand, you actually tell the compiler to pass the address of the variable to the function, rather than the value of the variable. The function then accesses the value of the variable by directly accessing the memory location.

Suppose you want to query the user for more than one data item. You would use the program in Listing 4.7.

Listing 4.7. Entering multiple data items with *scanf()*.

```
/***********************************************
  SCANF2.C - Inputting multiple items with scanf().
  Crash Course in C by Paul J. Perry
***********************************************/
```

```
#include <stdio.h>

int main()
{
  char name[20];
  int part;
  float cost;

  printf("Please enter name, part number, and cost\n");

  scanf("%s %d %f", &name, &part, &cost);

  printf("Name is: %s\n"
         "Part is: %d\n"
         "Cost is: %f\n",
           name, part, cost);

  return 0;
}
```


What follows is a sample interaction with the user:

```
Please enter name, part number, and cost
GinsuKnife 1234 19.95
Name is: GinsuKnife
Part is: 1234
Cost is: 19.950000
```

Notice that the user must separate the multiple data items by whitespace characters (Space, Tab, or Enter). You can see that the data items can continue to two or more lines because Enter is considered a whitespace character.

The individual data elements can also be entered as:

```
GinsuKnife
1234
19.95
```

or as:

```
GinsuKnife
1234 <tab> 19.95
```

whereby *<tab>* represents the user pressing the Tab key. The same information can even be input as:

```
GinsuKnife <tab> 1234 <tab> 19.95
```

I think you get the point. Because of this procedure, you cannot enter a string containing spaces in this same way. You have to use a *string input function* (as you will learn about later in this chapter).

As a programming technique, you can see in the second call to `printf()` that a long string can be separated on several lines by putting quotations around the string. The line in question is

```
printf(Name is: %s\n"
       "Part is: %d\n"
       "Cost is: %f\n",
       name, part, cost);
```

This same line can be entered like so:

```
printf("Name is: %s\nPart is: %d\nCost is: %f\n",
       name, part, cost);
```

Although this second form is acceptable, it is much easier for the programmer to read the first form. It is always desirable to have highly readable code.

String I/O Functions

There are two important functions that facilitate the transfer of strings between the computer and the standard I/O devices. They are the `gets()` and `puts()` functions. Their names represent *get string* and *put string,* and that is exactly what the functions do.

Each of these functions takes a single argument. The argument must be a character array (a string). The character array for the `puts()` function can include alphabetic, numeric, and any other special characters you might want to display.

Syntax at a Glance

String I/O with *gets()* and *puts()*

The `gets()` and `puts()` functions offer an alternative to the use of the `scanf()` and `printf()` functions for reading and displaying strings. The functions are declared like this:

```
gets(string)
```

and

```
puts(string)
```

The following lines show an example of `gets()` and `puts()` in action:

```
char str[255];
char msg[] = "This is a message";
gets(str);  /* get string from the user */
puts(msg);  /* display the message */
```

Take a look at an example program that shows how the `gets()` and `puts()` functions operate. Listing 4.8 reads a line of text into the computer and then writes it to the screen in its original form.

Listing 4.8. Reading and writing a line of text.

```
/************************************************
  STRINGIO.C - Example of string I/O functions.
  Crash Course in C by Paul J. Perry
 ************************************************/

#include <stdio.h>

int main()
{
   char text[255];

   puts("Enter a line of text\n");
   gets(text);

   puts("\n\nText Entered: ");
   puts(text);


   return 0;
}
```

Here is a sample interaction with the program:

```
Enter a line of text

a crash course in c taught me


Text Entered:
a crash course in c taught me
```

The program uses the `puts()` and `gets()` functions to write text to the display and to get character input from the user.

CAUTION

Be careful that the array you create is large enough to hold the string that is to be entered. If the array is not large enough, there is danger of a memory overwrite, because the compiler does not do any bounds checking for arrays.

Summary

In this chapter, you learned fundamental input and output operations. The chapter focused on the interaction between the computer and the monitor. In particular, the following important points were covered:

- The C language does not directly provide for input and output operations.
- Library functions must be used to access any type of I/O device, including the keyboard, the video display, the parallel printer port, the serial port, and any other I/O devices on your computer system.
- There are two types of input: *buffered* and *unbuffered.* Characters typed by the user that are stored in a temporary storage place until the user presses Enter are buffered input. Unbuffered input is sent, character-by-character, to the program as it is typed.
- C compilers provide several functions that perform character input and output.
- You learned how to get a single character from the user and display it on the video display with the `getchar()` and the `putchar()` functions.
- The C language declares several predefined streams for use in your programs. This enables you to automatically have access to the keyboard, the video display, the printer port, the serial port, and a standard error stream that is usually routed to the video display.
- You use the `scanf()` function to input formatted data. This function enables you to specify the type and format of data to be input. The function expects you to supply a format string argument specifying data types to input, and a list of addresses indicating where input data is to be stored.
- You use the `printf()` function to output formatted data. This function enables you to specify the type and format of data to be output. The `printf()` function expects you to supply a format string argument specifying data types to output, and a list of variables to be output.

CHAPTER FIVE

Programs that Make Decisions

The essence of any computer program is the decisions it can make and act on. Every day, humans must make decisions based on certain facts and then act appropriately. For example, if somebody knocks on the front door, you look to see who it is. If it is a friend, you will ask him or her in for a cup of coffee. However, if you see the newspaper carrier, you will get your wallet so you can pay the monthly newspaper bill.

The same sort of decision-making process occurs in computer programs. The program tests conditions and responds to stimuli depending on the results of the tests. Any computer program must make decisions to be useful. The *conditional statements* discussed in this chapter enable a program to make decisions and act on them.

The C programming language has three major decision-making statements: the `if` statement, the `if...else` statement, and the `switch` statement. Also, the `break` statement allows the decision-making statements to have more flexibility. This chapter examines the ways C uses these decision-making statements.

The *if* Statement

When deciding which statements to execute, the computer considers all the current conditions of your program. The `if` statement is the basic decision-making statement in C.

Syntax at a Glance

The Simple *if* Statement

The general form of the `if` statement is

```
if (expression)
    statement;
```

The `if` statement enables you to test an expression and act according to how the expression is evaluated. If *`expression`* evaluates to true (1), the computer executes the statement that follows. However, if *`expression`* evaluates false (0), *`statement`* is not executed. The *`expression`* part of the `if` statement is a relational test—covered in Chapter 3, "Variables and Operators."

If you have used another programming language such as Pascal or BASIC, you will notice that the `if` statement in C does not use the `then` keyword. If you try to slip it in, your C compiler will correct you with a message—`"undefined symbol 'then'"`. It then forces you to remove the undefined symbol before it compiles your program. The C language does not use the `then` keyword so to keep code notation lean and to the point.

For example, consider Listing 5.1, which plays a version of a guess-the-number game. You are prompted to enter a number. The program uses the equality operator (==) to determine whether your guess matches the constant `secretnumber` declared in the program. If you enter the right number, the program displays the message `"You guessed it!"`. If you do not enter the correct number, the program displays nothing.

Listing 5.1. Guess the number.

```
/*************************************************
  IF1.C - Sample program to demonstrate the
          if statement.
  Crash Course in C by Paul J. Perry
*************************************************/

#include <stdio.h>

int main()
```

```
{
   const int secretnumber = 21;
   int number;

   printf("Enter a number and try to "
          "guess the one "
          "I am thinking of: ");

   scanf("%d", &number);

   if (number == secretnumber)
      printf("\nYou guessed it!\n");

   return 0;
}
```

The `if` statement also can be displayed on one line, like this:

```
if(number == secretnumber) printf("\nYou guessed it!");
```

The idea of splitting the statement into two lines is to make it easier for people to read and understand.

CAUTION

When typing the listing, be careful not to type too many semicolons at the end of the line.

When typing the listing, be careful not to type too many semicolons at the end of the line. Especially notice the line that begins with the `if` statement. It does not end with a semicolon, as lines usually do. The reason the `if` statement does not contain an ending semicolon is because the line following it is actually part of the statement. If you add an extra semicolon, such as:

```
if(number == secretnumber);
    printf("\nYou guessed it!");
```

The `printf()` function is executed every time the program runs, regardless whether the variable named `number` is equal to the constant `secretnumber`. The terminating semicolon in the `if` statement informs the compiler that the conditional statement is complete; the next `printf()` statement is executed like a regular statement. This conventional notation causes beginning C programmers to pull their hair out when they find the problem after hunting laboriously through the program for an error.

NOTE

The `if` statement is not generally a true statement by itself—in the simple `if` statement in Listing 5.1, the `if` portion, `(if(number == secretnumber))`, is simply a clause of the rest of the statement, `(printf("\nYou guessed it!");)`.

Using Program Blocks with the *if* Statement

The body of the if statement can consist of a single statement followed by a semicolon (as was demonstrated earlier) or by a number of statements surrounded by braces.

Syntax at a Glance

The Block *if* Statement

The modified form of the `if` statement that executes a block of statements follows:

```
if (expression)
{
   statement1;
   statement2;
     .
     .
     .
   statementX;
}
```

The set of braces surround the multiple statements if the expression evaluates to true. There is no limit to the number of statements you can include inside an `if` statement when you use braces. It is important to always include the pair of matching braces. If you forget to include one brace, the compiler gets confused quickly.

What follows is Listing 5.2, which is a version of Listing 5.1, rewritten to display several lines of congratulations to the player who guesses the correct number.

Listing 5.2. Using program blocks in an *if* statement.

```
/************************************************
  CONGRAT.C - Guess the number with congratulations.
  Crash Course in C by Paul J. Perry
 ************************************************/

#include <stdio.h>

int main()
{
   const int secretnumber = 21;
   int number;

   printf("Enter a number and try "
          "to guess the one "
          "I am thinking of: ");

   scanf("%d", &number);

   if(number == secretnumber)
   {
      printf("\nYou guessed it!\n");
      printf("You must have special intelligence.\n");
      printf("Congratulations to you!\n");
   }

   return 0;
}
```


When CONGRAT.C is executed, the dialog with the user looks something like this:

```
Enter a number and try to guess
the one I am thinking of: 21

You guessed it!
You must have special intelligence.
Congratulations to you!
```

The multiple statements in the block are each terminated with a semicolon. The entire block is surrounded with braces. Using program blocks in an `if` statement allows the program to be more complex. This leads you to the next subject, that of nested `if` statements.

Nested *if* Statements

A nested `if` statement is an `if` statement that is included inside another `if` statement.

Syntax at a Glance

The Nested *if* Statement

The general format for the nested `if` statement is

```
if (expression)
       if (another expression)
    statement;
```

You will see that the second `if` statement is actually part of the body of the first `if` statement. The inner `if` statement is not executed unless the outer one evaluates to true. The *`statement`* is executed unless both `if` statements evaluate to true.

Listing 5.3 shows how to use nested `if` statements. This is a modification of the original guess-a-number program. This time, if you don't guess the correct number, the program informs you whether you guessed too high or too low.

Listing 5.3. Using nested *if* statements.

```
/********************************************
  IF2.C - Example of nested if statements.
  Crash Course in C by Paul J. Perry
 ******************************************/

#include <stdio.h>

int main()
{
   const int secretnumber = 21;
   int number;

   printf("Enter a number and try "
          "to guess the one "
          "I am thinking of: ");

   scanf("%d", &number);

   if(number == secretnumber)
      printf("\nYou guessed it!");

   if(number != secretnumber)
   {
      printf("Sorry, you didn't guess it...\n");

      if (number > secretnumber)
           printf("You guessed too high\n");
```

```
      if (number < secretnumber)
         printf("You guessed too low\n");
   }

   return 0;
}
```

The program checks whether the number the player guessed is not equal (using the `!=` operator) to `secretnumber`. If it is not, it checks whether the number is greater than or less than `secretnumber`. A message is then displayed depending on whether the number is greater than or less than `secretnumber`.

The *if...else* Statement

The `if` statement—by itself—is a powerful part of the C programming language that you can use to test expressions and take an appropriate action depending on the expression tested. The `if` statement executes a statement or group of statements when an expression evaluates to true. It does not take any action if the expression is false. This is where the `if...else` statement comes into action. The `if...else` statement allows a program to take a separate action if the expression does not evaluate to true.

Syntax at a Glance

The *if...else* Statement

The `if...else` statement is similar to the `if` statement. It adds an additional set of instructions, as follows:

```
if (expression)
  statement1;
else
  statement2;
```

The first two lines are the same as the original `if` statement. The `else` keyword signifies the statement to be executed if the expression does not evaluate to true.

To demonstrate the added power of the `if...else` statement, you can rewrite the number-guessing program, as shown in Listing 5.4.

Listing 5.4. Sample *if...else* Program.

```
/**********************************************
  IFELSE.C - Rewritten number-guessing game.
  Crash Course in C by Paul J. Perry
 *********************************************/

#include <stdio.h>

int main()
{
   const int secretnumber = 24;
   int number;

   printf("Enter a number and "
          "try to guess the "
          "one I am thinking of: ");
   scanf("%d", &number);

   if(number == secretnumber)
      printf("\nYou guessed it!\n");
   else
      printf("\nSorry, you didn't guess it\n");

   return 0;
}
```

See how the `if...else` statement simplifies the program? This program has a single `if...else` group of statements that either displays the message `"You guessed it!"` if you entered the correct number, or displays `"Sorry, you didn't guess it"` if the number was not equal to `secretnumber`.

All along, the example programs have tested different variables. You can also test a function because as you will learn, functions return values. The following example, Listing 5.5, tests the result of the `getchar()` function and displays a value depending on what the user enters.

Listing 5.5. Program that uses a function as an expression.

```
/************************************************
  IFELSE2.C - Sample program to use the result of
              a function call instead of testing
              an expression.
  Crash Course in C by Paul J. Perry
 ***********************************************/

#include <stdio.h>
```

```
#include <ctype.h>

int main()
{
   printf("Type a key on the keyboard: ");

   if ( toupper(getchar()) == 'Y')
      printf("\nYou pressed the Y key");
   else
      printf("\nYou did not press the Y key");

   return 0;
}
```

This example starts to show some of the power of the C programming language in testing the result of a function in an `if...else` statement. Notice the new function, `toupper()`, which converts a character to uppercase. It is defined in the CTYPE.H header file.

The `if` statement gets a character from the keyboard with a call to the `getchar()` function. It then converts that character to uppercase with the `toupper()` function and determines whether the character is equal to the letter *Y*. If the user typed the *Y* character (upper- or lowercase), the program makes the user aware of it. Otherwise, a message is displayed that informs the user that they did not press the *Y* key.

5

Nested *if...else* Statements

The `if...else` statement can be nested in the same manner as the `if` statement. However, you have to be careful because nested `if...else` statements have the potential for ambiguity. For example, consider the program, IFELSE3.C, in Listing 5.6.

Listing 5.6. Nested *if...else* example program.

```
/*****************************************
  IFELSE3.C - Nested if...else statements.
  Crash Course in C by Paul J. Perry
 *****************************************/

#include <stdio.h>

int main()
{
   int temp;
```

continues

Listing 5.6. Continued

```
   printf("Please enter the current "
            "room temperature\n");

   scanf("%d", &temp);

   if (temp < 85)
      if (temp > 65)
         printf("Sounds pretty comfortable.\n");
      else
           printf("Sort of chilly right now.\n");
   else
      printf("It is right now.\n");

   return 0;
}
```

The program nests two `if...else` statements. It asks the user to enter the current room temperature. If the temperature is less than 85, the program falls to the second `if` statement and checks whether the room temperature is greater than 65. If this is true (in which case the number the user entered is between 65 and 85), the program then displays a message `"Sounds pretty comfortable."`.

If the number is less than 65, the program displays the message `"Sort of chilly right now."`. Finally, if the number is greater than 85, the program falls to the final `else` statement, causing the computer to display the message `"It is hot right now."`.

You have to be careful when using nested `if` statements. For example, suppose you rewrote the code to look like this:

```
if (temp < 85)
   if (temp > 65)
      printf("Sounds pretty comfortable.\n");
else
      printf("Sort of chilly right now.\n");
   else
   printf("It is right now.\n");
```

The actual code did not change, it is only formatted differently. It now seems that the first `else` statement belongs to the first `if` statement. However, the compiler still interprets the code in the same way. This inconsistency leads to problems that are difficult to track down. Remember, the way you format a program does not make any difference to the compiler. It uses certain rules for compiling the code. These rules are constant and are used all the time.

> **NOTE** The moral of the story is that the C programming language always associates an `else` with the closest preceding `if` statement.

In Listing 5.6, the code is formatted to make it obvious as to what should occur (or at least partly obvious). Don't allow the code formatting to confuse you as to a statement's purpose. Incorrectly formatted code creates a logical error that can be difficult to track down.

> **CAUTION**
>
> Don't use too many `if...else` statements—nested `if...else` statements have the potential for ambiguity. Too many of these will only confuse you and possibly introduce a logical error.

The *switch* Statement

You can make some decisions using the `if` or `if...else` statements. Sometimes, however, the resulting code can be difficult to follow and can confuse even an advanced programmer. The C programming language has a built-in, multiple-branch decision statement called `switch`. The `switch` statement causes a particular group of statements to be chosen from several available groups. The `switch` statement is similar to the `if...else` statement, but has increased flexibility and a clearer format.

Syntax at a Glance

The *switch* Statement

The `switch` statement is similar to the `case` statement in Pascal or the `Select...Case` statement in Microsoft QuickBASIC. BASICA and GWBASIC don't have an equivalent statement.

The general form of the `switch` statement is as follows:

```
switch (expression)
{

   case constant1 :
      statement1;
      break;
```

The *switch* Statement Continued

```
   case constant2 :
      statement2;
      break;

   case constant3 :
      statement3;
      break;
         .
         .
         .
   case constantX :
      statementX;
      break;

   default :
      default statement;
}
```

In the `switch` statement, the computer tests a variable consecutively against a list of integer or character constants. After finding a match, the computer executes the statement or block of statements that are associated with the specified constant.

The `default` statement is executed if the compiler does not find a match in the list of constants. The `default` statement is optional. If `default` is not present and all matches fail, no action takes place. When finding a match, the computer executes the statements associated with the specified case until it reaches the `break` statement or the end of the `switch` statement.

Following each of the `case` keywords is an integer or character constant. This constant ends with a colon (not a semicolon). There can be one or more statements following each `case` keyword. The statements are not required to be enclosed in braces. However, the entire body of the switch statement must be enclosed in braces.

Listing 5.7 shows you how to use the `switch` statement to process keyboard commands (like those in a menu program). The program displays a menu on-screen and prompts the user to enter a value.

It then displays a status message. In a real menu program, you would use a function call to execute the appropriate command, thus accomplishing the request of the user.

Listing 5.7. Sample program using the *switch* statement.

```
/*******************************************
  MENU.C - Show use of the switch statement.
  Crash Course in C by Paul J. Perry
 ******************************************/

#include <stdio.h>

int main()
{
   char ch;

   printf(" ***Main Menu***\n");
   printf("1. Word Processor\n");
   printf("2. Spreadsheet\n");
   printf("3. Database\n");
   printf("\n");
   printf("Your Choice: ");

   ch = getchar();

   switch (ch)
   {
      case '1' :
           printf("\nExecuting Word processor\n");
           break;

      case '2' :
           printf("\nExecuting Spreadsheet\n");
           break;

      case '3' :
           printf("\nExecuting Database\n");
           break;

      default :
           printf("\nInvalid menu selection\n");
   }

   return 0;
}
```

Notice the use of the `break` statement at the end of each `case`. If you do not use the `break` statement, program flow continues to the next `case`. When several conditions use the same piece of code, continuing to the next `case` is helpful. Sometimes, the capability of the `cases` to run together when no `break` statement is present enables you to write more efficient programs by avoiding duplication of code. Most the time, however, this is not what you want to happen.

Listing 5.8 demonstrates how to use more than one `case` statement with a set of instructions.

Listing 5.8. Another program using *switch* statements.

```
/*************************************************
  SWITCH.C - Sample program using switch statements.
  Crash Course in C by Paul J. Perry
 *************************************************/

#include <stdio.h>

int main()
{
   char ch;

   printf("Do you wish to continue "
            "program execution (Y/N) ? ");

   ch = getchar();

   switch (ch)
   {
      case 'y' :
      case 'Y' :
           printf("\nThe answer was YES\n");
           break;


      case 'n' :
      case 'N' :
           printf("\nThe answer was NO\n");
           break;

      default :
           printf("\nWrong answer.\n");
   }

   return 0;
}
```

This program shows a common case (no pun intended) in which you have to respond to a letter selection from the user (`Y` for yes or `N` for no), yet you don't want to force the user to type the letter in a specific case. The SWITCH.C program uses the same code to process the key, whether the user entered the value in upper- or lowercase.

As you progress in your study of the C language, you will learn other ways to convert letters and methods from uppercase to lowercase and vice versa. For now, the previous programs give good examples of the `switch` statement.

Nested *switch* statements

As with the `if` and `if...else` statement, the `switch` statement can be nested. When you nest the statement, the `switch` statement is part of the statement sequence of an *outer* switch (the first `switch` statement). Even if the `case` constant of the inner `switch` and the outer `switch` contain common values, no conflicts arise.

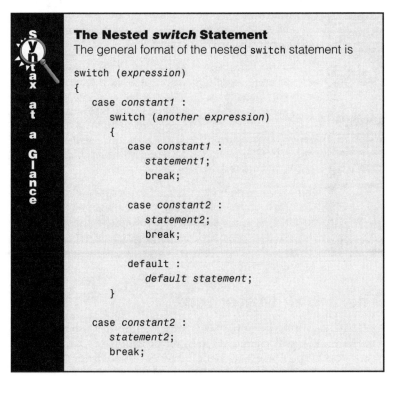

Syntax at a Glance

The Nested *switch* Statement

The general format of the nested `switch` statement is

```
switch (expression)
{
   case constant1 :
      switch (another expression)
      {
         case constant1 :
            statement1;
            break;

         case constant2 :
            statement2;
            break;

         default :
            default statement;
      }

   case constant2 :
      statement2;
      break;
```

The Nested *switch* Statement Continued

```
    case constant3 :
        statement3;
        break;
         .
         .
         .
    case constantX :
        statementX;
        break;

    default :
        default statement;
}
```

This general form probably looks familiar, because it is simply a `switch` statement inside another `switch` statement. The expression used for each `switch` statement is usually different.

The `switch` statement is a powerful element of the C programming language—it is actually the core statement used in advanced graphical operating environments such as OS/2 and Microsoft Windows. Although programming for this environment is a topic of its own, the core of most every program written for OS/2 and Microsoft Windows has a `switch` statement, usually nested with other `switch` statements.

The `switch` statement responds to messages from the user. For example, if the user presses the mouse button, the `switch` statement receives a message. The program then responds to the message appropriately.

The *break* Statement

You have seen the use of the `break` statement to exit the `switch` statement. You will see it used in other programs in Chapter 6 in more detail. The `break` statement transfers control from the `switch` statement to the first statement following the `switch` statement. It can be used also inside an `if` or `if...else` statement.

Summary

You have studied the three fundamental decision-making statements in the C programming language. The next chapter takes an equally important look at programs that loop.

> **NOTE** If you have typed the example programs in this chapter and feel comfortable with the material presented, continue your exploration of the C programming language. Otherwise, examine the example programs a little closer. Either way, take a break and pick up the book tomorrow—after a well-deserved rest.

The following points were covered in this chapter:

- The three decision making statements in the C programming language are the `if` statement, the `if...else` statement, and the `switch` statement.
- The `if` statement is the fundamental decision-making statement in the C programming language. It enables your program to test an expression and execute a statement or group of statements depending on the outcome of the test.
- The `if` statement can be used to execute a block of statements by surrounding the block with braces.
- A program can nest `if` statements by including an `if` statement inside another `if` statement. This allows for expanded decision-making capabilities.
- The `if...else` statement is an expanded version of the `if` statement. It takes action whether the expression is true or false.
- The `if...else` statement can be nested just like the `if` statement can. When doing so, you must be careful to match the right `else` with the right `if` statement.

  The rule to remember is that the C programming language always associates an `else` with the nearest preceding `if` statement.
- The `switch` statement causes a particular group of statements to be chosen and executed from several available groups. It also can cause several `case`s to use the same code, resulting in a more efficient use of your program's resources.

- Because of the flexibility of the C programming language, the `switch` statement can be nested similarly to `if` and `if...else`. When this occurs, the `switch` statement is part of the statement sequence of a `switch` statement.
- The `break` statement transfers control from a `switch` statement to the first subsequent statement in the program.

CHAPTER SIX

Programs that Loop

The last chapter focused on the decision-making statements available in the C programming language. Just as important as the decision-making statements are the *program-flow statements,* which you learn in this chapter.

In C programs, instructions are usually executed in the order in which they appear in a listing, from the beginning. Each instruction is executed once and only once. Programs of this type are not flexible or practical, because they do not include logical control structures.

It is the program-flow statements that allow a computer to continuously repeat a repetitive task without getting bored or tired. You can instruct a program to repeat a task any number of times. The computer does not whine, get cranky, or talk back.

Many programs require that a group of instructions be executed repeatedly, until a logical condition has been satisfied. This condition is known as *looping.* Sometimes the number of repetitions required is not known in advance, other times it is. You can have a situation in which a loop continues until a logical condition becomes true. All these operations can be executed with different types of looping statements—available in the C programming language.

Looping statements are used to control program flow. One of the chief strengths of a computer is its capability to perform repeated tasks rapidly, accurately, and without complaint. You can instruct the computer to do the same thing over and over again, millions of times, if necessary.

There are three major program loop statements in the C programming language: the `for` loop, the `while` loop, and the `do...while` loop. Each of them is discussed in turn. You will also learn the different varieties of each type of loop, as well as examine other statements used in the three main looping constructions.

The *for* Loop

The `for` loop is the fundamental looping statement in C. It is often used for situations in which you want to execute a task a specific number of times. The `for` loop is the statement you use for this job—it appears in almost every programming language available. However, C gives you more power and flexibility (which means more complexity) than most languages.

Syntax at a Glance

The *for* Loop

The general form of the `for` statement is

```
for (initialization; condition; increment)
     statement;
```

The parentheses following the keyword `for` contain the necessary elements for the `for` statement. The *`initialization`* keyword is used to initialize an index parameter that controls looping action. The *`condition`* represents a condition that must be satisfied in order for the loop to continue execution. Finally, *`increment`* is a value that determines how much the index variable is incremented.

The body of the `for` loop is located in the statement section. You can use braces to enclose multiple statements, or list a single statement (as shown).

```
int x;
for (x=0; x<10; x++)
   printf("This will be displayed 10 times\n");
```

CAUTION

A common error when writing `for` loops is to place a semicolon between the loop expressions and the body of the loop. Don't do it. The result does not create a complex C statement, and therefore will not compile.

To get you started, Listing 6.1 gives an example of a simple `for` loop. The listing displays the numbers from 1 to 100 on-screen.

Listing 6.1. Example *for* loop program.

```
/****************************************
  FORLOOP.C - Simple for loop example.
  Crash Course in C by Paul J. Perry
 ****************************************/

#include <stdio.h>

int main()
{
   int x;

   for (x=1; x<=100; x++)
      printf("Iteration: %d \n", x);

   return 0;
}
```

This program declares an integer index variable called `x`. The core functionality of the program lies in the `for` loop:

```
for (x=1; x<=100; x++)
```

The loop initially sets the variable `x` to 1. The second part of the `for` statement checks whether `x` is less than or equal to 100. If `x` passes this test, the program calls the `printf()` function, which displays the iteration number. After the number is displayed on-screen, the program increments the variable `x` by 1, using the increment operator (++). The statement could easily have appeared like this:

```
for (x=1; x<=100; x=x+1)
```

This looping process repeats until `x` is greater than 100, at which time the loop terminates and the program ends.

There is no law that says that the loop is required to always run in a positive direction. You can create a program that counts down simply by changing the increment operator. For example, Listing 6.2 is a modification of the earlier program. It counts down from 100 to 1 on-screen.

Listing 6.2. Example *for* loop that counts down from 100.

```
/**************************************
  COUNTDN.C - Counts down from 100 to 1.
  Crash Course in C by Paul J. Perry
 **************************************/

#include <stdio.h>

int main()
{
   int x;

   for (x=100; x>0; x—)
      printf("%d \n", x);

   return 0;
}
```

These two programs just begin to show the versatility of the `for` statement. Notice that the decrement (—) operator is used in this example. The control variable is initialized to 100, then the program determines whether the variable is greater than 0. If it is greater than 0, the body of the loop displays the value of `x`. For each test, if the variable `x` is greater than 0, the loop continues executing. Finally, when `x` becomes 0, the loop is terminated and the program ends.

C does not restrict you to incrementing or decrementing the value of the control variable by one. You can use any type of assignment operator. For example, the next program (TENCOUNT.C) in Listing 6.3 prints the numbers from 0 to 100, counting by 10 (0, 10, 20, 30, and so on).

Listing 6.3. Program to count to 100, by 10.

```
/********************************************
  TENCOUNT.C - Displays numbers from 0 to 100,
               counting by 10.
  Crash Course in C by Paul J. Perry
 ********************************************/
```

```
#include <stdio.h>

int main()
{
   int x;

   for (x=0; x<=100; x=x+10)
      printf("The variable x is equal to %d \n", x);


   return 0;
}
```

Notice that a C program has complete control of incrementing the control variable. A control variable can be modified in the loop, but it is usually considered poor style. However, the compiler does enable you to do so. Also, remember that any test can be used inside the condition section of the `for` statement. For example, the statement:

```
for (x=3; x==25; x++)
   printf("x=%d", x);
```

starts the loop by initializing the variable `x` to the value 3. The loop continues as long as `x` is equal to 25. For each time through the loop, `x` is incremented by one (with the increment operator). Unfortunately, this is a useless loop statement. The reason being that the code following the `for` statement will never be executed. Your program never allows `x` to equal 25, therefore the `printf()` function in this code is never executed.

6

NOTE The moral of the story is that, although you have great flexibility with `for` loops, you also have to be careful with the values you pass to the statement. If not, unexpected results can occur. For example, if you have a statement like:

```
for (x=11; x<10, x++)
  printf("this will never be displayed\n");
```

the body of the loop will not be executed. The reason is because *x* starts at 11 and is incremented. At the same time, the code executes the body of the loop only when *x* is less than 10. Therefore, nothing happens. These statements are a waste of memory—the body of the loop is never executed.

The ANSI C standard does not require any statement to follow the `for` statement. This means that the body of the `for` loop can be empty. You can use this fact to create time delays in your code. For example, this statement:

```
for (t=0; t< 999; t++)
    ;
```

causes the program to sit in a loop while the variable `t` counts from 0 to 999. No statements are executed, but the computer will be busy crunching numbers. As mentioned, this is a quick and dirty method for creating a time delay.

If you are working with real-time programming, be careful. The above loop will take different amounts of time to execute on different computers. An obvious example is if you compile the program on a PC computer, and then recompile the source code on a Cray supercomputer. Execution speeds will be drastically different, resulting in a different delay.

All the preceding examples have used a single statement in the body of the loop. It is possible for more than one statement to be used in the `for` loop by enclosing the block of statements in curly braces ({ and }). The following program (AVG.C) in Listing 6.4 calculates the average of five, user-entered numbers.

Listing 6.4. Loop to calculate the average of five numbers.

```
/*********************************************
  AVG.C - Averages five numbers entered by user.
  Crash Course in C by Paul J. Perry
 *********************************************/

#include <stdio.h>

int main()
{

   int counter;
   const int max = 5;
   float x, average, sum = 0;

   printf("This program will prompt you ");
   printf("for five numbers\n");
   printf("It will then display the ");
   printf("average of these five numbers\n\n");

   for (counter=1; counter<=max; counter++)
```

```
    {
       printf("\nEnter number value of %d: ", counter);
       scanf("%f", &x);
       sum = sum + x;
    }

    average = sum / max;

    printf("\nThe average of the "
           "numbers is %f", average);


    return 0;
}
```

The program in Listing 6.4 uses the `for` statement to prompt the user to type five numbers. Each time through the loop, the program prompts the user to enter a value. The program then stores the value in `x` and adds the value to the running total stored in the variable `sum`. After the loop ends, the program divides the variable `sum` by the number of values entered (the integer constant `max`, equal to 5). Finally, the program displays the results to the user before the program terminates.

The important element of Listing 6.4 was the use of braces around the three statements that form the body of the `for` loop:

```
for (counter=1; counter<=max; counter++)
{
   printf("\nEnter value of number %d : ", counter);
   scanf("%f", &x);
   sum = sum + x;
}
```

This group of statements, from beginning brace to ending brace, is treated as a single statement by the compiler. Notice that each statement in the block is a C statement and must be terminated with a semicolon. However, the entire block is not terminated with a semicolon.

The C programming language allows several variations that increase the power of `for` loops even more. One of the more common variations is the capability to use two or more control variables. The following program (TWOVARS.C) in Listing 6.5 shows how two variables are initialized at the same time in the initialization section of the `for` statement.

Listing 6.5. Sample of initializing several variables in a *for* loop.

```
/*********************************************
  TWOVARS.C - Initializes several variables
              in a for loop.
  Crash Course in C by Paul J. Perry
 *********************************************/

#include <stdio.h>

int main()
{
   int counter, total;

   for (counter=0, total=0; counter<=100;
     counter=counter + 10)
   {
      total = total + 1;
      printf("counter = %d and total = %d\n",
          counter, total);
   }

   return 0;
}
```

When the program in Listing 6.5 is executed, the output looks something like this:

```
counter =  0 and total = 1
counter = 10 and total = 2
counter = 20 and total = 3
counter = 30 and total = 4
counter = 40 and total = 5
counter = 50 and total = 6
counter = 60 and total = 7
counter = 70 and total = 8
counter = 80 and total = 9
counter = 90 and total = 10
counter = 100 and total = 11
```

The variables `counter` and `total` are both initialized inside the `for` loop statement. Although the variable `total` was not used as an index variable in the loop, it can still be initialized at the beginning of the loop. This is one of the nice things about C—it does not force you to use any specific style. As mentioned before, C gives you lots of flexibility.

The output of the program displays the value of the counter, as well as the number of times the loop was executed.

Nested *for* Statements

Just as decision-making statements can be nested, so can program-flow statements. A nested `for` statement includes a `for` statement in another `for` statement. To demonstrate this structure, Listing 6.6 presents a short program that displays a multiplication table.

Syntax at a Glance

The nested *for* Loop

The general form of the nested `for` loop is

```
for (initialization; condition; increment)
{
   for (initialization; condition; increment)
   {
      statement1;
      statement2;
      statement3;
      ...
      statementN
   }
}
```

Listing 6.6, which follows, contains an example of a nested `for` statement.

Listing 6.6. Nested *for* statement that displays a multiplication table.

```
/*******************************************
  MTABLE.C - Displays a multiplication table.
  Crash Course in C by Paul J. Perry
 *******************************************/

#include <stdio.h>

int main()
{
   int column, row;

   for (row=1; row<=10; row++)
   {
      for (column=1; column<=10; column++)
```

continues

Listing 6.6. Continued

```
            printf(" %5d", column * row);
        printf("\n");
    }

    return 0;
}
```

The program displays a table that looks something like this:

```
 1   2   3   4   5   6   7   8   9  10
 2   4   6   8  10  12  14  16  18  20
 3   6   9  12  15  18  21  24  27  30
 4   8  12  16  20  24  28  32  36  40
 5  10  15  20  25  30  35  40  45  50
 6  12  18  24  30  36  42  48  54  60
 7  14  21  28  35  42  49  56  63  70
 8  16  24  32  40  48  56  64  72  80
 9  18  27  36  45  54  63  72  81  90
10  20  30  40  50  60  70  80  90 100
```

This multiplication table is suitable for teaching youngsters multiplication and is available for framing in a variety of sizes. The secret behind creating the table is in the nested `for` loop statements.

The numbers in the left column and top row serve as the labels of the multiplication table. If you go to the intersection point of a row and a column, you find the sum of the two numbers. For example, start at 6 on the top column and go down seven rows to the intersection of 6 and 7. You find the number 42, because 6 multiplied by 7 is equal to 42.

Listing 6.6 creates two loops: an inner loop and an outer loop. The inner one steps through 10 columns, from 1 to 10, while the outer loop steps through 10 rows. For each row, the inner loop executes once, then a carriage return is displayed so to prepare for the next line of the table.

Each time through the inner loop—at the intersection of each column and row—the program multiplies the two numbers and displays the product in the table. To make sure the columns line up correctly, a field-width specifier of four is used in the `printf()` function.

CAUTION

The rule for nested `if` statement applies equally well to nested `for` loops—a program block is associated with the closest preceding `for` statement. Don't allow program formatting to convince you that incorrect sections of your code will be executed.

You have examined several different variations of the `for` loop. Notice that each `for` loop requires that you always perform the conditional test at the beginning of the loop. This means that the program will never execute the code inside the loop if the condition tested is false. Next, you will study some program-flow structures that enable you to control when the test is executed.

The *while* Loop

The second type of loop available in the C programming language is the `while` loop.

Syntax at a Glance

The *while* Loop

The general form of the while statement is

```
while (expression)
    statement;
```

An example follows:

```
while (x == TRUE)
    printf("The variable x is TRUE");
```

The reserved word `while` is followed by an expression surrounded by parentheses. The statement can be a single statement followed by a semicolon or a block of statements surrounded by braces.

In the `while` loop, the body of the loop is executed as long as the expression is true. When the expression becomes false, program control passes to the line that follows the loop.

Listing 6.7 shows a program that produces similar results to Listing 6.1 except it uses the `while` statement. It counts from 1 to 100, displaying the numbers on-screen.

Listing 6.7. Sample program using the *while* loop.

```
/**************************************************
  WHILE.C - Example of counting from 1 to 100.
  Crash Course in C by Paul J. Perry
 **************************************************/

#include <stdio.h>

int main()
{

   int counter = 1;

   while (counter <= 100)
   {
      printf("Iteration: %d\n", counter);
      counter++;
   }

   return 0;
}
```

Listing 6.1 has many of the same elements of the simple program that demonstrated the `for` statement. Notice how you would initialize an index variable (`counter`) and increment it in the loop.

The program can be written more precisely, as follows:

```
#include <stdio.h>

int main()
{
   int counter = 1;

   while (counter <= 100)
      printf("Iteration: %d\n", counter++);

   return 0;
}
```

When executed, this program generates the same output as the first, however it is several lines shorter. As is usual with the C programming language, you can produce the same results with fewer code instructions. Instead of incrementing the index value as a statement, the second example shows it as part of the `printf()` function call. By doing this, the programmer can use a single statement as the target of the `while` loop.

You can easily argue that either looping method—the `for` statement or the `while` statement—is easier to use. Each statement has its own place and time that it should be used. Many times these statements can be used interchangeably, as you have just seen.

Take a look at a different type of example. Listing 6.8 (TYPE0.C) loops until the user types the number 0.

Listing 6.8. Sample program that quits when user presses zero key.

```
/********************************************
  TYPE0.C - Demonstrates the while loop.
  Crash Course in C by Paul J. Perry
 ********************************************/

#include <stdio.h>

int main()
{
   int x = 1;

   while (x != 0)
   {
      printf("Enter a number, type 0 to quit\n");
      scanf("%d", &x);
   }


   return 0;
}
```

The TYPE0.C program does not know how many times the user will type a number other than 0. Therefore, the `while` loop continues to loop until a certain condition is met. As long as the user does not type 0, the loop continues to be executed.

The `while` loop differs from the `for` loop in that there is no initialization section for the `while` statement. The initialization must be done separately—as is shown in Listing 6.8 when `x` is initialized to 1. It can be initialized to any variable other than 0 and the program will still work. The initialization is to make sure that the number is not 0, in which case the loop would never execute.

Listing 6.9 uses a `while` loop to check each character in a string. If the character is the null-terminating character, you exit the loop. You can then determine how long the string is.

Listing 6.9. Program that finds the number of characters in a string with the *while* loop.

```
/**************************************************
  COUNT.C - Counts number of characters in a string.
  Crash Course in C by Paul J. Perry
 **************************************************/

#include <stdio.h>

int main()
{
   int count = 0;
   char str[255];

   printf("Type in a word :\n");
   scanf("%s", &str);

   while (str[count] != '\0')
      count++;

   printf("\nThe word was %d "
          "characters long\n", count);

   return 0;
}
```

Here is a sample interaction with the program:

```
Type in a word :
CisForMe

The word was 8 characters long
```

The program uses the `scanf()` function to query the user to type a string. It then counts how many characters are in the word. A `while` loop is used to start at the beginning of the string and count until a terminating null character is found (`\n`). The program than reports the number of characters in the word. Notice that the string must not be separated by spaces because the `scanf()` function would interpret the space as the beginning of a new string.

Nested *while* Loops

Just as `for` loops can be nested, so can `while` loops. By now you know what is meant by the term *nested.* Nested `while` loops enable you to put a `while` loop inside another `while` loop.

Syntax at a Glance

Nested *while* Loops

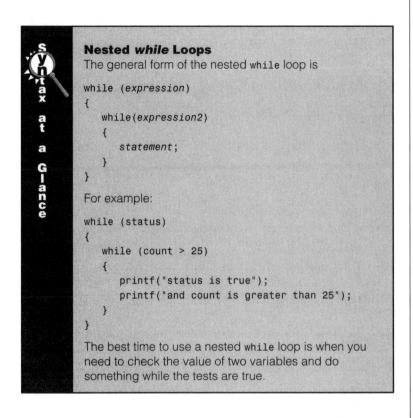

The general form of the nested `while` loop is

```
while (expression)
{
   while(expression2)
   {
      statement;
   }
}
```

For example:

```
while (status)
{
   while (count > 25)
   {
      printf("status is true");
      printf("and count is greater than 25");
   }
}
```

The best time to use a nested `while` loop is when you need to check the value of two variables and do something while the tests are true.

The *do...while* Loop

The last type of loop in C is the `do...while` loop. This loop structure is similar to the `while` loop. Unlike the `for` and `while` loops, which test the loop condition at the top of the loop, the `do...while` loop checks its condition at the end of the loop. This means that a `do...while` loop will always execute at least once.

The `do...while` loop, unlike the other loop statements you have examined, has two keywords: `do` and `while`. The `do` keyword marks the beginning of the loop. The `while` keyword marks the end of the loop and contains the loop expression. Notice that the `do...while` loop is terminated with a semicolon.

Syntax at a Glance

The *do...while* Loop

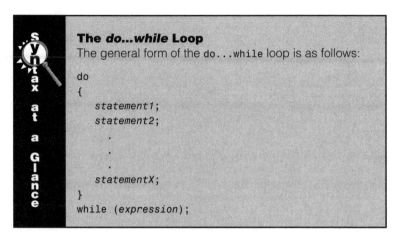

The general form of the `do...while` loop is as follows:

```
do
{
    statement1;
    statement2;
        .
        .
        .
    statementX;
}
while (expression);
```

The statements enclosed in braces will be executed repeatedly, as long as the value of expression is true (not equal to zero). The curly braces ({ }) are required when working with a block of statements—the `do...while` loop is almost always used with a block of statements.

NOTE Although curly braces are not necessary in the `do...while` loop when only a single statement is present, they are frequently used to improve the overall readability of the statement.

Listing 6.10 is equivalent to Listing 6.1, except it uses the `do...while` loop construction to display the numbers from 1 to 100.

Listing 6.10. Program that counts from 1 to 100 with the *do...while* loop.

```
/***************************************
  DOWHILE.C - Sample do...while loop.
  Crash Course in C by Paul J. Perry
 ***************************************/

#include <stdio.h>

int main()
{
```

```
   int x = 1;

   do
   {
      printf("%d\n", x++);
   }
   while ( x <= 100);

   return 0;
}
```

The important point to notice about this program is that the body of the loop will always be executed at least once because the test condition is at the end of the loop. If you are familiar with the Pascal programming language, you may think that the `do...while` loop is similar to the `repeat...until` statements. The difference is that the `repeat...until` statement loops until the test condition is true, whereas the `do...while` loop continues to loop while the test condition is true.

For most applications, it is more natural to test for continuation of the loop at the beginning rather than at the end of the loop. For this reason, the `do...while` statement is used less frequently than the other looping statements covered.

Arrays and Loops

Looping structures are an ideal method for quickly accessing array elements. Because an array has an index value, a loop can be used to increment through each element of the array. Listing 6.11 shows an example.

6

Listing 6.11. Program that moves through an array with loops.

```
/***********************************************
  LOOPS.C - Example of using loops with arrays.
  Crash Course in C by Paul J. Perry
 ***********************************************/

#include <stdio.h>
#include <limits.h>

int main()
{
   int numbs[10], count, avg;
```

continues

Listing 6.11. Continued

```
    int total = 0, smallest = INT_MAX, largest = 0;

    /* introduction */
    printf("This is a program to average numbers.\n");
    printf(" You will be asked for 10\n");
    printf("numbers.\n\n");

    /* Get the 10 numbers */
    for (count=0; count<10; count++)
    {
       printf("Please enter number %d: ", (count+1) );
       scanf("%d", &numbs[count]);
       total = total + numbs[count];
    }

    /* Calculate average */
    avg = total/10;

    /* Find the largest and smallest numbers */
    /*   by going through the entire array   */
    /*   using a do...while loop.             */
    count = 0;
    do
    {
       if (numbs[count] > largest)
            largest = numbs[count];

       if (numbs[count] < smallest)
            smallest = numbs[count];

       count++;
    }
    while (count<10);

    /* display output to user */
    printf("\n\nResults\n"
        "———\n");

    printf("The average value is %d\n", avg);
    printf("The numbers added equal %d\n", total);
    printf("The largest number "
           "entered was %d\n", largest);
    printf("The smallest number "
           "entered was %d\n", smallest);

    return 0;

}
```

Here is a sample interaction with the program:

```
This is a program to average numbers.
You will be asked for 10
numbers.

Please enter number 1: 5
Please enter number 2: 10
Please enter number 3: 15
Please enter number 4: 5
Please enter number 5: 10
Please enter number 6: 15
Please enter number 7: 5
Please enter number 8: 10
Please enter number 9: 15
Please enter number 10: 10

Results
-------
The average value is 10
The numbers added equal 100
The largest number entered was 15
The smallest number entered was 5
```

The program gets 10 numbers from the user and then displays information about those numbers to the user, including the average value, the sum of the numbers, the largest number entered, and the smallest number entered. The program uses a `for` loop to go through the array and prompt the user for the numbers.

The code to get the values from the users looks like this:

```
for (count=0; count<10; count++)
{
   printf("Please enter number %d: ", (count+1) );
   scanf("%d", &numbs[count]);
   total = total + numbs[count];
}
```


Notice that `printf()` adds 1 to the `count` variable. The reason for this is that arrays in C always start at index 0, yet it would be odd for a program to ask the user to "enter number 0". This is why the program adds 1 to the numeral displayed to the user.

The `scanf()` function reads the value into the current array element. A variable named `total` determines the total of the sum of all numbers entered. After the user enters all the numbers, the average value is calculated by subtracting the total sum from the total number of entries.

A `do...while` loop is then used to find the largest and smallest number. Another `for` loop could have been used, but it was a good opportunity to show the use of a different type of statement. Finally, the program uses a series of `printf()` statements to display the findings of the program.

Infinite Loops

Infinite loops are loops which continue forever. The only way to stop a program that has an infinite loop is to abort the program in an unnatural way. Some compilers have a special option for break checking. When break checking is on, the compiler will check for the press of the Break key in the program and terminate the program if the Break key is pressed. If your compiler does not have break checking, the only way to end a program that has an infinite loop is to restart the computer.

Infinite loops are useful at times to force a program to continue running for an extended length of time. The infinite loop is a quick way to force the instructions to be repeated several times.

To create an infinite loop with the `for` statement, don't use any value for the three control variables. For example:

```
for (;;;)
     printf("this will continue to print forever\n");
```

To do the same thing with a `while` loop, use code like this:

```
while (1)
{
   printf("this will continue to print forever\n");
}
```

and finally, to accomplish an infinite loop in a `do...while` loop, write code that looks like this:

```
do
{
   printf("this will continue to print forever\n");
}
while (1);
```

Exiting an Infinite Loop

You could write your own code to exit out of an infinite loop, using C's `break` statement, first introduced in Chapter 5. Whenever the `break` statement is encountered anywhere inside the body of a loop, it causes immediate program termination. For example, you could rewrite a `for` loop to look like this:

```
char ch;

for (;;;)
{
   printf("this will continue to print forever\n");
   printf("unless you press the letter 'A' now\n");
   scanf("%c", &ch);
   if (ch=='A')
      break;
}
```

This loop will continue to run until you type `A` in response to the message. If you press any other key, the program continues to loop.

Labels and the *goto* Statement

If you are familiar with programming with any language, you might be surprised to see the "dreaded" `goto` statement showing up in a language as prestigious as C. The use of the `goto` statement is looked at by many programmers as an inferior style of coding. The reason is that it leads to poorly structured programs.

However, the designers of the C programming language included the `goto` statement because, in their own words "there are a few situations in which `goto` may find a place."

The problem with programs that use the `goto` statement is that the code is generally harder to understand and to update than code written without `goto` statements. That is why it is looked down on by many programmers.

Syntax at a Glance

The *goto* Statement

The goto statement is used to alter the normal sequence of program execution by transferring control to some other part of the program. In its general form, the goto statement is written as follows:

```
goto label;
```

whereby *label* is an identifier used to label the target statement that will receive the control. The target statement must be labeled, and the label must be followed by a colon. Each statement in the program must have a unique label. No two statements can have the same label. The target statement appears as:

```
label:

  statement;
```

For example:

```
int main()
{
label:
   printf("X");
goto label;
```

This example creates an infinite loop that repeatedly displays the letter *X* on-screen.

CAUTION

Make sure that each statement in your goto program has a unique label. No two statements can have the same label; if there are two statements with the same label, the compiler will issue an error message.

Listing 6.12 shows how to use the goto statement in a program.

Listing 6.12. Program that uses the *goto* statement.

```
/*******************************************
  TRYGOTO.C - Example of the goto statement.
  Crash Course in C by Paul J. Perry
*******************************************/
```

```
#include <stdio.h>

int main()
{
   int counter = 0;

try_again:

   if (counter > 100)
      goto stop;

   printf("%d\n", counter);
   ++counter;
   goto try_again;

stop:

   return 0;
}
```

Listing 6.12 counts from 0 to 100. If you compare this program to Listings 6.1 and 6.7, you will probably find that this program is not as easy to understand. Execution is not smooth because it jumps from location to location.

NOTE Avoid using the `goto` statement—use instead an appropriate looping statement. In every case, you should be able to find a more elegant method using one of the looping structures. Because the `goto` statement creates unstructured programs, you will not see it used in any other place in this book.

The *break* Statement

The `break` statement has several uses. Its first purpose was to terminate a `case` statement, as you learned in Chapter 5. Its second purpose is to force immediate termination of a loop, therefore bypassing the normal loop conditional test.

When the compiler encounters the `break` statement inside a loop, the computer terminates the loop and program control resumes at the statement that follows the loop. Take a look at Listing 6.13.

Listing 6.13. Program that uses the *break* statement.

```
/*******************************************
  TRYBREAK.C - Example of the break statement.
  Crash Course in C by Paul J. Perry
 *******************************************/

#include <stdio.h>

int main()
{
   int x;

   for (x=0; x<100; x++)
   {
      printf("variable x equals %d\n", x);
      if (x==10)
           break;          /* exit loop */
   }

   return 0;
}
```

The output of this program looks like this:

```
variable x equals 0
variable x equals 1
variable x equals 2
variable x equals 3
variable x equals 4
variable x equals 5
variable x equals 6
variable x equals 7
variable x equals 8
variable x equals 9
variable x equals 10
```

The program prints the value of the variable, from 0 to 10, then terminates. This occurs because the `break` statement causes immediate exit from the loop. The break statement overrides the conditional test `x<50`. It is important to understand that a `break` statement will cause an exit from the innermost loop only. For example, the following:

```
for (x=0; x<50; ++x)
{
   count = 1;
   for(;;;)
   {
      printf("count is %d\n", count);
      count++;
```

```
      if (count==10)
         break;
   }
}
```

displays the values of count 1 through 10 on-screen 100 times. Each time that the computer encounters the `break` statement, the program passes control back to the outer `for` loop.

> **NOTE** The `break` statement exits from the innermost loop only. The next outer loop receives control after the `break` is done executing.

The *continue* Statement

The `continue` statement is used to bypass the remainder of a pass through a loop. It executes similarly to the `break` statement. However, instead of forcing termination, `continue` forces the next iteration of the loop to take place and skips any code in between.

The `continue` statement can be used with program-flow statements as well. The `continue` statement works similarly to the `break` statement. However, instead of forcing loop termination, the `continue` statement forces the next iteration of the loop to take place, and skips any code in between. For example, take a look at Listing 6.14.

Listing 6.14. Example of the *continue* statement.

```
/*******************************************
  CONTIN.C - Example of continue statement.
  Crash Course in C by Paul J. Perry
 *******************************************/

#include <stdio.h>

int main()
{
   int x;

   for (x=0; x<50; x++)
```

continues

Listing 6.14. Continued

```
    {
        if (x%2)
            continue;
        printf("variable x equals %d\n", x);
    }

    return 0;
}
```

Program output looks like:

```
variable x equals 0
variable x equals 2
variable x equals 4
variable x equals 6
variable x equals 8
variable x equals 10
variable x equals 12
variable x equals 14
variable x equals 16
variable x equals 18
variable x equals 20
variable x equals 22
variable x equals 24
variable x equals 26
variable x equals 28
variable x equals 30
variable x equals 32
variable x equals 34
variable x equals 36
variable x equals 38
variable x equals 40
variable x equals 42
variable x equals 44
variable x equals 46
variable x equals 48
```

Each time that the program generates an odd number, the `if` statement executes because an odd number modulus 2 is always true. Therefore, an odd number causes the `continue` statement to execute, which causes the next iteration to occur, bypassing the `printf()` function and only displaying the even numbers.

The `continue` statement works a little differently in `while` and `do...while` loops. In this case, the `continue` statement causes program control to go directly to the conditional test and then continue the looping process. In the case of the `for` loop, the computer first performs the increment part of the loop. Then the computer performs the conditional test, all before the loop continues.

The `continue` statement can be used to quicken the termination of a loop by forcing the computer to perform a conditional test as soon as it encounters some terminating condition.

Summary

In this chapter, you focused on program-flow statements. You learned the commands used in the C programming language to direct the flow of a program. You also learned the three basic program control statements and how they are used. Specifically, the following important points were covered:

- There are three basic program control statements in the C programming language. They are the `for` loop, the `while` loop, and the `do...while` loop.
- The `for` loop is the fundamental looping statement in C. It can have a single statement terminated by a semicolon or a block of statements surrounded by braces as its body. You can also nest the `for` statement. The `while` statement is used in a program in which you do not know how many times the loop will have to execute.
- The `do...while` statement is similar to the `while` statement, except that its logical test is at the end of the loop. Therefore, the body of the loop is always executed at least once.
- The `goto` statement is included in the C language because sometimes it is the only way out of a certain condition. However, the `goto` statement should not be relied on to change program flow. It results in the creation of unstructured programs.
- The `continue` statement forces the next iteration of the loop to take place and skips any code in between.
- Each of the three program-control statements can be nested in themselves. When the statement is nested, it means that another loop is embedded in the outer loop.

CHAPTER SEVEN

Modular Programming with Functions

Functions are the core of the C programming language. It is because of functions that C is extensible and expandable. In this chapter, you'll examine the syntax, format, and purpose of functions. You learn about the standard library of functions included with every ANSI C compiler. Most importantly, you learn how to use functions to convert your programs into logical units that fit together like a puzzle.

The Concept of Functions

A *subprogram* is an important concept associated with a high level programming language. Subprograms, or *functions,* as they are called in the C programming language, are the basis of all heavy-duty computer programming languages. Programmers who have used Pascal, FORTRAN, and modern versions of BASIC should already be familiar with functions.

Pascal uses functions and procedures. The C programming language does not have the concept of *procedures* (a subprogram that returns no value). All subprograms are called functions. However, you can inform your program that your function does not return a value. Therefore, C functions have the capabilities of *both* functions and procedures in Pascal.

A *structured program* is one that consists of subprograms that create a working program when combined. All programs written today are made up of subprograms. A function is simply a means of separating program logic into small parts.

The idea behind a function is separating each section of code that performs a specific task and treating it as a separate entity. Then, whenever you have to accomplish the task that the function carries out, you simply call the function. A function can be called as many times as is necessary.

A function is given its own name and accessed by that name. Data can be passed to a function, on which the function then operates. In the beginning of this book, you were introduced to functions. The `main()` function definition of every program is considered a function to which the operating system passes control when a program starts running.

You have already used the built-in *library functions,* except you might not have guessed they were functions. These general-purpose functions come with the compiler. Examples of library functions include `printf()`, `scanf()`, `gets()`, and `puts()`. In fact, there are a great number of functions included with the standard definition of the C language. These library functions are not considered parts of the C programming language.

The ANSI C definition provides a summary of *standard functions*—functions that should be included as standard on all ANSI-compatible C compilers. This way, one is assured that all C compilers have a base set of functions that act in the same manner and style.

In fact, most C compilers add a great number of functions on top of those standard functions. These "extended" functions support the basic features of the computer on which they are running. For example, both Borland and Microsoft C compilers, which are only available on PC-based systems, include their own graphics libraries. These graphics libraries provide functionality for accessing graphics capabilities inherent to the PC system. Other compilers on different computers probably use completely different functions for their graphics routines.

> **NOTE** The unfortunate aspect of these libraries is that there is no standardization among manufacturers on the function names for these extended libraries. Therefore, a program that uses extended graphics functions on one compiler cannot be ported to a different system and be quickly recompiled.

Using the Standard Library

The standard C function library provides routines for the most common programming tasks. The standard library functions provide a convenient interface to the language and a base level of functionality.

The function library is divided into smaller, related groups. For examples, the time library includes functions for working with the date and time and the standard I/O library includes functions that control input and output on the computer.

To use the functions in your own programs, all you have to do is include the appropriate header file at the beginning of your program. The header file contains the declarations of the functions. The standard library functions are executed by declaring their names. This can be done by including the appropriate header file at the beginning of the program. For example,

```
#include <math.h>
```

enables you to use the mathematical functions. The MATH.H file is inserted in your program and includes declaration for the available math functions.

> **NOTE** Remember that the `#include` statement is a preprocessor directive that informs the compiler to merge the specified header file into your source file during compilation. The included file is referenced when your program is being compiled.

The angle brackets surrounding the header filename tell the compiler to look in the standard library directory. In the previous example, the file included is the MATH.H header file. This file is used for standard input and output. You have already used library functions for many tasks in your programs up to this point—using the function library should not be an entirely new concept.

The definitions for the standard library are divided among 15 header files. Each header file is responsible for a specific group of functionality. Table 7.1 lists the header files and the types of functions they declare.

Table 7.1. Header files included in the standard C library.

Header File	*Description*
ASSERT.H	Allows diagnostics to be added to programs.
CTYPE.H	Declares functions for testing characters.
ERRNO.H	Defines constants for error conditions.
FLOAT.H	Defines constants for floating-point arithmetic.
LIMITS.H	Defines constants for sizes of data types.
LOCALE.H	Includes functions that provide country and language information.
MATH.H	Defines mathematical functions.
SETJMP.H	Provides a way to change program flow with functions.
SIGNAL.H	Includes functions for handling exception conditions.
STDARG.H	Provides facilities for variable argument lists.
STDDEF.H	Defines common data types and macros.
STDIO.H	Provides facilities for standard input and output.
STDLIB.H	Defines utility functions.
STRING.H	Includes functions for working with character arrays.
TIME.H	Includes date and time functions.

Although the C standard library definitions are split among 15 header files, they can be divided into 10 main categories. They are

- *Input and output.* Functions that handle the tasks of moving data in and out of your programs.
- *String and character.* Functions that manipulate characters and character arrays (strings).
- *Mathematical.* These functions handle many of the common mathematical calculations you might need.
- *Time and date.* These functions handle time and date functions as related to the operating system.
- *General utilities.* This is a group of basic C programming utility functions.
- *Character-handling.* These functions test character variables.
- *Diagnostics.* These functions enable you to troubleshoot bugs in your programs.
- *Nonlocal jumps.* These functions provide ways to avoid normal function call and return sequences.
- *Signal-handling.* These functions handle *exception conditions,* such as an interrupt signal or an error condition.
- *Variable length argument lists.* These functions enable an unknown number of variables to be passed to a function.

Now, take a brief look at each group of functions and explore how they are used.

Input and Output Functions

The input and output (I/O) functions represent almost one third of the entire standard C library. The input and output functions declared in STDIO.H provide functions for the standard I/O devices (as listed in Table 7.2) and file I/O. The STDIO.H header file also declares file input and output. Both sequential and random-access file I/O is provided for—you examine them in Chapter 11.

Table 7.2. Standard streams declared in STDIO.H.

Stream Name	*Description*	*Device*
stdin	Input stream	Keyboard
stdout	Output stream	Video display
stdprn	Printer stream	Printer port
stdaux	Auxiliary output	Serial port
stderr	Error stream	Video display

String and Character Functions

The STRING.H header file declares functions that manipulate character arrays. Unlike other programming languages, which have a predefined string variable type (like BASIC), C does not have any explicit string type. Instead, all programs that use a group of characters also use character arrays (as you already know).

Because C does not have a string type, you cannot assign the value of one string to another. For example, the following code is invalid:

```
char a[99];
char b[99] = "Cannot do this";

a = b;  /* illegal operation */
```

Instead, a program has to make use of functions that copy the contents of one string to another string. Instead of using the above assignment statement, a C program uses code that looks something like this:

```
#include <string.h>

char a[99];
char b[99] = "This can be done";

strcpy(a, b);  /* Copy contents of variable b to variable a */
```

The STRING.H header file contains functions that are useful for comparing strings, finding the length of strings, and manipulating strings. Table 7.3 lists some of the most important string-manipulation functions available in the standard C string library.

Table 7.3. String-manipulation functions.

Function	*Description*
`strcmp()`	Compares two strings
`strlen()`	Returns length of a string
`strcat()`	Appends one string to another
`strcpy()`	Copies one string to another

Mathematical Functions

The header file MATH.H declares mathematical functions. These functions provide functionality beyond basic addition, subtraction, multiplication, and subtraction.

You will find trigonometric functions defined, functions for finding the square root of a number, and functions for finding the logarithm of a number. There are also several other miscellaneous functions for mathematical operations. Table 7.4 lists the most common functions.

Table 7.4. Mathematical functions.

Function	*Description*
`abs()`	Absolute value of an integer variable
`fabs()`	Absolute value of a floating-point number
`sin()`	Sine of a number
`cos()`	Cosine of a number
`tan()`	Tangent of a number
`asin()`	Arc sin of a number
`acos()`	Arc cosine of a number
`atan()`	Arc tangent of a number
`log()`	Natural logarithm
`log10()`	Base 10 logarithm
`exp()`	Exponential function
`sqrt()`	Square root function
`pow()`	The power of a number

Although the mathematical functions provide a good base level of math capability, you might need more powerful math functions for specialized scientific or statistical programs. In this case, you have the choice of writing your own functions or purchasing third-party math libraries. These libraries are available with a number of different capabilities and varying costs. Evaluate several of them before making a firm decision as to which one to use.

Time and Date Functions

The TIME.H header file declares types and functions for manipulating the date and time. The main functions declared in the header file enable to you to get the current system date and time from the operating system. The functions support several different time formats. There are also functions for converting among time formats.

On UNIX-based machines, the date and time is expressed by the number of seconds elapsed since 00:00:00 hours Greenwich Mean Time (GMT) on January 1, 1970. This is a universal representation of the time. Some of the important functions for working with the time and date are listed in Table 7.5.

Table 7.5. Time and date routines.

Function	*Description*
`stime()`	Sets the system's time and date
`time()`	Gets the time in Greenwich Mean Time (GMT)
`asctime()`	Converts time from one data type to another
`clock()`	Returns elapsed processor time in clicks

General Utility Functions

The functions declared in STDLIB.H provide functions that every C program will use. These include common data types, number conversion, and memory storage allocation. Table 7.6 lists some of the most common functions declared in the STDLIB.H header file.

Table 7.6. General utility functions declared in STDLIB.H.

Function	*Description*
`rand()`	Returns a random number
`srand()`	Returns random number from a seed
`exit()`	Causes program to terminate
`abort()`	Causes program to terminate abnormally
`malloc()`	Allocates memory
`realloc()`	Reallocates memory
`free()`	Returns allocated memory to the system
`system()`	Executes an operating-system function
`qsort()`	Sorts an array using the quick sort algorithm

Character-Handling Functions

The CTYPE.H header file declares functions for testing characters. These are useful for determining what type of value is stored inside a `char` (character) variable. For example, the `isupper()` function returns a true value if the specified character is uppercase. The `isdigit()` function returns true if the number is a decimal digit. Table 7.7 lists some of the more useful character-handling functions.

Table 7.7. Character-handling functions.

Function	*Description*
`isalpha()`	Determines whether a character is alphabetic
`iscntrl()`	Determines whether value is a control character
`islower()`	Determines whether a character is lowercase
`ispunct()`	Determines whether a value is a punctuation character
`isspace()`	Determines whether value is a space character
`isupper()`	Determines whether character is uppercase
`islower()`	Determines whether character is lowercase
`tolower()`	Converts character to lowercase
`toupper()`	Converts character to uppercase

Diagnostics Functions

Although most compilers provide debugging tools, such as stand-alone debuggers, the C language defines functionality in the ASSERT.H header file for adding diagnostics services to a program. There is only one function declared and it is named (appropriately enough) `assert()`.

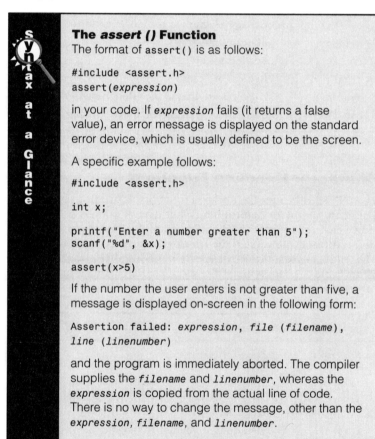

Syntax at a Glance

The *assert ()* Function

The format of `assert()` is as follows:

```
#include <assert.h>
assert(expression)
```

in your code. If *`expression`* fails (it returns a false value), an error message is displayed on the standard error device, which is usually defined to be the screen.

A specific example follows:

```
#include <assert.h>

int x;

printf("Enter a number greater than 5");
scanf("%d", &x);

assert(x>5)
```

If the number the user enters is not greater than five, a message is displayed on-screen in the following form:

```
Assertion failed: expression, file (filename),
line (linenumber)
```

and the program is immediately aborted. The compiler supplies the *`filename`* and *`linenumber`*, whereas the *`expression`* is copied from the actual line of code. There is no way to change the message, other than the *`expression`*, *`filename`*, and *`linenumber`*.

Although there are more user-friendly ways to assure that the value entered by the user is valid, when you are testing variables dependent on hardware, the `assert()` function is a handy method for checking for error values.

Nonlocal Jump Functions

Like the diagnostic functions, there are only several functions declared in the SETJMP.H header file. The `setjmp()` function provides a way to avoid a normal function call and return sequence. Usually, it is used to permit an immediate return from a deeply nested function.

Signal-Handling Functions

Many programs are written to handle system interrupts. The C programming language provides facilities for processing these interrupts in the SIGNAL.H header file. It is functions like these that give C its power. Most high-level languages don't provide any way for handling system interrupts. The C programming language is one of the exceptions.

When you declare a signal handler, you use the `signal()` function. You provide the type of interrupt you want `signal()` to handle, as well as the name of the function that you want `signal()` to call. The ANSI definition declares three types of interrupts that you can set. Table 7.8 lists the type of signal you can set and what that interrupt does.

Table 7.8. Types of signal handlers a C program can set.

Value	*Description*
SIG_DFL	Terminates the program
SIG_ERR	Indicates error return from signal
SIG_IGN	Ignores this signal type

7

Variable Argument List Functions

Variable length argument lists allow several values to be passed to a function. Whereas some functions can take only one parameter, like `puts()`, others can take any number of parameters. For example, `printf()` can take several parameters, depending on the contents of its first string, as shown in the following examples:

```
printf("number is %d", i);
                          /* two parameters */
printf("name is %s, number is %d", str, i);
                         /* three parameters */
```

The C programming language provides you with the capability to write functions that take a different number of arguments. Variable-length argument lists are unique to C. To declare variable-length argument lists, you must include the STDARG.H header file.

Now that you have learned the standard functions included with most C compilers, you will learn how to write your own functions. This way, you can unleash the power of C because all the functions you write are considered to be equal to the standard library functions. Therefore, when you write functions, you are actually extending the language. This enables you to develop features and functions that the developers of C never thought of or needed.

A Simple Function

As was previously defined, a function is a self-contained program in another program that carries out a specific, well-defined task. A program can contain multiple functions, each considered a separate program.

Several reasons for using functions are that they aid in the overall organization of a program, they reduce the memory overhead required by the compiler, and they enable you to create reusable code. By dividing tasks into logical, well-defined functions, program organization is improved. This aids the programmer working on a team, as well as the one working alone on a project.

The second important aspect of functions is their capability to reduce the memory required in a program. By calling a function instead of repeating the code every time a task has to be executed, a program uses less memory. Although computers can now be expanded to 16M (megabytes) of memory and beyond, creating memory-efficient programs is still a priority for most developers.

Finally, functions enable you to reuse code. Reusing code can save you many hours of programming time. This refers to the capability to separate a program into well-defined tasks that compose the functions. Then, you can use these functions for more than one programming project.

For example, almost every program that uses disk files must have a section of code that asks the user for a filename and determines whether the file is present on the disk. By putting this task into a function, you eliminate a piece of code you must write for your next program. As a result, programmers tend to build up large libraries of their favorite routines, enabling the programmers to create new applications quicker.

Declaring the Function

The function carries out its intended action whenever it is accessed (or whenever the function is "called" from another portion of the program). The same function can be accessed from several different places in a program. Once the function has carried out its intended action, control returns to the point at which the function was accessed.

NOTE A function usually contains three parts: the *function declaration,* the actual *function,* and the *function call.*

Syntax at a Glance

Function Declarations

Just as you can't use a variable without first informing the compiler what it is, you also can't use a function without informing the compiler about it. The function is usually declared at the beginning of the program. The program declaration takes the following general form:

```
type function_name(type varname1,
         type varname2,
         ...,
         type varnameX);
```

The declaration informs the compiler that, at some point in the program, you plan on creating a function with the name `function_name`. The first `type` keyword informs the compiler what data type the function returns. Any C data type can be specified. If the function is not to return any value, you use the keyword `void`.

The list of types and variable names in parameters are the arguments that are passed to the function. A function can be used without parameters, in which case the parameter list will be empty, however the parentheses are still required. The function declaration ends with a semicolon.

Function Declarations Continued
The following is a code example of a function declaration:

```
function void foo(int x);   /* declaration */
void foo(int x)
{
   printf("The value is %d" x);
}

int main()
{
   foo(3);
   return 0;
}
```

It is important to point out that, unlike a variable declaration in which many variables can be declared of a common type at once, such as:

```
int dollars, cents, total;
```

all function parameters must include both the type and variable name. For example, this is the correct parameter declaration for the above variables when used as arguments to a function:

```
int dollars, int cents, int total
```

The Function Body

The second step to using a function is writing the body. The general form is as follows:

```
type function_name(type varname1,
                   type varname2,
                   ..., type varnameX)
{
  /* body of function */
}
```

The first line of the function is virtually a copy of the function declaration, except it is not followed by a semicolon. Again, the rule applies that all parameters must include both the type and variable name. The statements that form the body of the function are enclosed in braces.

> **NOTE** Don't make the common mistake of placing a semicolon after your function declaration. Doing so will introduce a bug into your program!

Calling the Function

Once the function is written, you can use it in your program. Here is an example of how a function is used in a program:

```
void main()
{
  /* other statements */

  function_name(var1, var2, ..., varX);

  /* more statements */

}
```

If you wish to use the value returned by a function, you would put the function on the right side of an assignment statement, as follows:

```
value = function_name(var1, var2, ..., varX);
```

Listing 7.1 is an example of a program that uses a simple function.

Listing 7.1. Program that uses a basic function.

```
/***************************************************
  SIMPFUNC.C - A simple function used in a program.
  Crash Course in C by Paul J. Perry
 ***************************************************/

#include <stdio.h>

void showdashes(void);    /* function declaration */

int main()
{
   printf("This is to be underlined\n");
   showdashes();     /* function call */
   printf("Hey, do that once again\n");
   showdashes();     /* function call */
   return 0;
}
```

continues

Listing 7.1. Continued

```
/***********************/
void showdashes()
{
   printf("------------------------\n");
}
```

When the program is executed, it displays four lines of output, as follows:

```
This is to be underlined
------------------------
Hey, do that once again
------------------------
```

Notice that the function was called twice, thereby saving the hassle of typing the code twice as well as the memory required to store it twice.

The function above, named `showdashes()`, is the simplest type of function a C program can use. It doesn't return a value and is not passed any values from the main program. Although the simple function may help organize a program, in order for functions to be useful, you must be able to receive values from a function and pass values to them.

Functions that Return a Value

Some functions, like `showdashes()`, don't return any data, whereas other functions can return values. The `return` statement is used to return a value from a function.

The `return` function actually has two uses. First, it causes an immediate exit from the current function. That is, program flow returns to the statement located after the function call. Second, it is used to return a value to the program.

Program execution in a function usually ends when the compiler finds the closing brace in the function. You can force a function to return to the calling program at a specific point by using the `return` statement.

To return a value from a function, you must follow the `return` statement with the value to be returned. For example, this function returns the absolute value (removes the negative sign) of a number.

```
int absolute(int number)
{
  int result;
  if (number>1) return number;
      /* If number is positive, return now. */

  result = -number;
     /* Make number positive. */

  return result;
}
```

Listing 7.2 is a full-blown example of using the function in a program.

Listing 7.2. Program to return a value from a function.

```
/**************************************************
  RETVAL.C - Example program that returns a
             value from a function.
  Crash Course in C by Paul J. Perry
 **************************************************/

#include <stdio.h>

int absolute(int number);  /* function declaration */

int main()
{
   printf("%d\n", absolute(9) );  /* Test function */
   printf("%d\n", absolute(-9) );
   printf("%d\n", absolute(0) );

   return 0;
}


/**************************************/
int absolute(int number)  /* body of function */
{
   int result;
   if (number>0)        /* Is number positive? */
      return number;    /* If so, return now */

   result = number - number - number;
                        /* Make it positive */

   return result;
         /* Return value to calling function. */

}
```

The `main()` section of the program feeds a couple of numbers into the function to make sure it works. The output of the program is as follows:

```
9
9
0
```

If it does not come out this way, you should check the program to make sure everything was entered correctly.

Each time the function is called, it is passed an integer value. Inside the function, this value is referred to as the variable `number`. However, because functions are considered separate program modules, you could have a variable with the same name in `main()` and the compiler would access it as if it was a variable with a different name.

Inside the function, a test is made to determine whether the value passed to the function is positive. If it is, the function does not have to do anything; it returns to the calling program immediately using the `return` statement. The calculation makes the number positive by calculating the inverse of the number (`-number`).

The result of the calculation is then returned to the main program with the `return` statement followed by the value to be passed back (in this case, the variable `result`).

Passing Data to a Function

The information to be passed to a function is called an *argument* (also called a parameter).

Now that you have returned data from a function, you should learn how to pass data to a function. The last program gave you a sneak preview of how it is done. Once you have declared the data types of the argument in the program, you can access them with the specified variable name. Listing 7.3 (PASSDAT.C) is an example of a function that is passed two numbers and returns the sum of the numbers.

Listing 7.3. Function to add two numbers.

```
/**************************************************
  PASSDAT.C - Pass data to a function with arguments.
  Crash Course in C by Paul J. Perry
 **************************************************/

#include <stdio.h>

/* Function declaration */
int add(int num1, int num2);

int main()
{
   int result;
   result = add(1, 2);
   printf("1 + 2 is %d", result);

   return 0;
}


/******************************/
int add(int num1, int num2)
{
   int result;  /* Local variable  */

   result = num1 + num2;
               /* Actual calculation  */

   return result;

}
```

Although this function uses integer parameters, you could rewrite the function to use any of the regular data types. The output of the program is

```
1 + 2 is 3
```

The program shows how multiple variables are used in the function. Notice that the variable declared as `result` is called a *local variable.* What this means is that the variable is used only in the function. If you tried to make access to the variable in `main()`, the compiler would report an error. Later in this chapter, you learn methods of sharing variables throughout functions and programs.

Passing Arrays to a Function

You have seen how to pass standard data types to a function. This section shows how to pass arrays to your functions.

Passing Arrays

The following program in Listing 7.4 uses a bubble sort to sort an array of numbers. It is an example of passing an integer array to a function.

Listing 7.4. Bubble sort routine.

```
/***************************************
  SORT.C - Sort an integer array.
  Crash Course in C by Paul J. Perry
 ***************************************/

#include <stdio.h>

void sort(int list[]);  /* function declaration */

const int MAX = 10;

int main()
{
   int count = 0, list[10];

   printf("You will be prompted for 10 numbers.\n");

   do
   {
      printf("Enter number %d: ", count+1);
      scanf("%d", &list[count++]);
   }
   while (count < MAX);

   sort(list);

   printf("\n\nResults\n");

   for (count=0; count<MAX; count++)
      printf("Position %d is now %d\n",
              count, list[count]);

   return 0;
}

/*********************************/
void sort(int list[])
```

```
{
   int i, j, temp;
   for (i=0; i<MAX-1; i++)
   {
      for (j=i+1; j<MAX; j++)
      {
      if (list[i] > list[j])
      }
         temp = list[j];
         list [j] = list[i];
         list [i] = temp;
      }
      }
   }
}
```

Output of the program looks similar to this:

```
You will be prompted for 10 numbers.
Enter number 1: 4
Enter number 2: 7
Enter number 3: 4
Enter number 4: 2
Enter number 5: 687
Enter number 6: 322
Enter number 7: 1
Enter number 8: 67
Enter number 9: 9
Enter number 10: 23

Results
Position 0 is now 1
Position 1 is now 2
Position 2 is now 4
Position 3 is now 4
Position 4 is now 7
Position 5 is now 9
Position 6 is now 23
Position 7 is now 67
Position 8 is now 322
Position 9 is now 687
```


The sorting algorithm is based on a bubble sort, whereby the lower numbers move slowly to the top of the list. It is an inefficient algorithm, but simple to implement. The function, named `sort()`, is passed an array of numbers. This function then sorts the list.

This program may seem strange after the earlier discussion of returning values. A function can only return a standard data type. You cannot return an array directly. This program simply takes the array as an argument, then rearranges the array.

Nothing is ever returned because the actual addresses of the array are passed to the function. Passing the array to the function does not create a new copy of the array. Unlike local variables, which are separate between functions, the array is one and the same. When you modify the array in the function, you are actually modifying the original array.

The designers of C decided it was a good idea to pass arrays this way because creating an entirely new array would use a large portion of memory as well as consume a lot of processor time.

Visibility and Lifetime of Variables

Any variable declared inside a function can be used only by statements inside the function. If you declare a variable outside of the functions, it is accessible by all the functions in the program. Variables that can be accessed by all functions are called *global variables.*

Listing 7.5 is an example of a program that uses both local variables (those variables inside a function) and global variables (those functions declared for all functions in a program).

Listing 7.5. Program to show some uses of global and local variables.

```
/************************************************
  GLOBAL.C - Demonstration of global and
             local variables.
  Crash Course in C by Paul J. Perry
 ************************************************/

#include <stdio.h>

void functioncall(void);    /* function declaration */

int number;                 /* global variable */

int main()
{
   printf("starting main()\n");
   number = 10;
   printf("number is %d\n", number);
   functioncall();
   printf("number is %d\n", number);
   return 0;
}

/****************************/
void functioncall()
```

```
{
   number = 25;
   printf("returning from function\n");
}
```

The output of the program looks like this:

```
starting main()
number is 10
returning from function
number is 25
```

This example creates a global variable, named `number`. It is first assigned the value 10 in `main()`. A function then assigns 25 to the variable. The value of the variable is displayed several times during execution of the program so you can see how the variable changes.

CAUTION

Certain care should be taken when declaring and using global variables. You should try to avoid making all your program's variables global. Otherwise, you will start creating functions that rely on certain global variables. The result is the functions cannot be used with other programs.

Although global variables can be handy, stay away from defining and using global variables unless absolutely necessary because they cannot be used with other programs. Worst yet, if you have a global variable and it is inadvertently modified by one function, other functions may react illogically. This is because the other functions expected the global variable to have a certain value. This is a difficult bug to detect.

The *main()* Function

You have seen the `main()` function declared many times by now. It looks like this:

```
int main()
```

This declaration says that the function returns an integer value. The value is used by the operating system to return an error condition. A zero value returned to the operating system means no errors occurred.

You can also specify other parameters to be passed from the operating system to the `main()` function when your program is first called. These parameters are called *command-line arguments.*

Command-Line Arguments

Command-line arguments are parameters that follow the program's name on the command line. For example, you can usually start an editor and specify the file to edit at the same time. This is done with the following line, entered at an operating system command-line prompt:

```
EDIT filename
```

whereby *filename* is the name of the file you want to edit. Many other programs enable you to do this trick. The operating system automatically passes any command-line parameters to the program being loaded.

Command-line arguments are usually used to pass information to a program when it runs. Command-line parameters are passed to a program as parameters of the `main()` function.

This is the *only* time you use the parentheses following the `main()` function. (Haven't you wondered what they were used for?) The general form when accessing command-line arguments is

```
void main(int argc, char *argv[])
 {
 .
 .   /* variables are used in body of program  */
 .
 }
```

Two built-in arguments are used to receive command-line arguments. They are `argv[]` and `argc` and are the only arguments that `main()` can have.

The `argc` parameter (short for *ARGument Count*) is an integer that holds the number of arguments passed on the command line. The `argv` parameter (short for *ARGument Values*) is a pointer to an array of character pointers. You have not yet learned pointers. All you have to know about them at this point, however, is that each element in the `argv[]` array corresponds to a command-line argument.

NON ANSI C STANDARD:

```
Void MAIN (ARGC, ARGV)
INT ARGC;
CHAR **ARGV;
{
```

Listing 7.6 displays the number of command-line parameters passed to the program as well as each command-line parameter.

Listing 7.6. Program to display command-line arguments.

```
/************************************************
  COMLINE.C - Access command-line arguments.
  Crash Course in C by Paul J. Perry
 ************************************************/

#include <stdio.h>

int main(int argc, char *argv[])
{
   int counter;

   printf("Number of arguments: %d\n", argc);

   for (counter=0; counter<argc; counter++)
      printf("Argument %d is %s\n",
          counter, *(argv+counter) );

   return 0;
}
```

If you invoke Listing 7.6 by typing:

`COMLINE this is a test`

the program should output something like this:

```
Number of arguments: 5
Argument 0 is C:\COMLINE.EXE
Argument 1 is this
Argument 2 is is
Argument 3 is a
Argument 4 is test
```

By convention, the first array element of `argv[]` is always the full pathname of the program being executed. As a result, `argc` is the number of command-line arguments, plus one.

Being able to pass command-line arguments to a program is helpful to the user, because she can start the program and specify a filename all at one time. As you can see, it is not difficult to add this functionality to your program.

Summary

This chapter discussed how to use functions. You learned the syntax, the format, and the purpose of functions. You also learned about the standard library that comes with C compilers. In particular, the following important points were covered:

- A function is a subprogram, or a program inside a program. Each function has its own variables, separate from the rest of the program.
- Functions are used to divide a program into logical units.
- Several reasons to use functions include the increase in organization of a program, the reduction in memory size, and the capability to reuse program code.
- Library functions are general-purpose functions that accompany the compiler. The ANSI C language definition provides for certain libraries as a base, which all compilers should support. These libraries are called the standard libraries.
- Data can be passed in and out of functions. You also learned how to pass arrays among functions.
- The `return` statement is used to pass a single value from the function to the line that called the function.
- The variables passed to a function are called arguments or parameters. They provide a means to pass information to the function.
- Global variables are variables that are declared outside of any function and can be accessed by all functions in a program.
- Command-line arguments are characters appearing after a program name at an operating system command prompt. They are accessed from a C program using the `argc` (for argument count) and `argv[]` (argument values) parameters from the `main()` function.
- The first command-line argument returned as `argv[0]` is always the full pathname of the program. Multiple arguments are separated on the command line with spaces. To include characters separated with spaces, enclose the string in quotations.

CHAPTER EIGHT

Preprocessor Directives

You can include various instructions for the C compiler in the source code of your program. These instructions, processed before the code is compiled, are called *preprocessor directives.* Preprocessor directives expand the scope of C beyond its basic definition. All preprocessor directives begin with the pound (#) character.

The preprocessor directives are interpreted before the compilation process begins. Preprocessor directives usually appear at the beginning of a program and are grouped together with other directives (although this is not required). The directives apply to the portion of the program following their appearance.

You have seen the line

```
#include <stdio.h>
```

in most of the programs in this book. This line instructs the compiler to include information about the standard input/output library. If you look at the STDIO.H file, you see that it looks like program code that would appear in your own program. This line appears at the beginning of most C source-code files.

The `#include` directive is only one of many preprocessor directives available. Others provide for macro definitions, conditional compilation, error generation, and line control. This chapter takes a look at these preprocessor directives and examines how you can use them in your own programs.

File Inclusion

As you have seen, file inclusion is one of the most common preprocessor directives used in the C programming language. When a file is *included,* the contents of the include file are inserted at the current location of the source file.

Syntax at a Glance

The *#include* Directive

The general form of file inclusion is

```
#include <filename.h>
```

The `#include` directive instructs the compiler to include another source file in the one that has the directive. The source file to be included is enclosed in angle brackets.

Another form of file inclusion follows the following format:

```
#include "filename.h"
```

This form, which uses quotations around the filename, instructs the compiler to search the current directory for the file to be included. You must include the full pathname and the extension of the file. The following example illustrates `#include`:

```
#include <stdio.h>
int main()
{
    printf("this function is in stdio.h");
    return 0;
}
```

NOTE In C, the file to be included in your code (in this case STDIO.H) is called a *header file,* or *header* for short. This naming convention is due to the fact that these declarations are usually found at the beginning of a program.

The angle brackets cause the preprocessor to search the default include file directory. This is usually a default of the compiler and depends on what type of system and what C compiler you are using.

> **NOTE** The first style of file inclusion (with angle brackets) is used for standard header files. These header files are declared for the standard C library. The second style of file inclusion (with quotations) is normally used for header files that are specific to a program.

Header files are usually reserved for function prototypes, variable declarations, and other preprocessor directives. Header files don't usually contain source code. The most common use of header files is for *function prototypes* (described in more detail in Chapter 7).

Macro Definitions

If file inclusion is the most common C preprocessor directive you encounter, macro definitions are probably the second most common. Macro definitions are usually associated with a word processor or spreadsheet. Macros save you time in carrying out your tasks. The C programming language includes its own macro facility.

Macros are part of the C preprocessor. That is, they are processed before the C compiler compiles the code. When the preprocessor encounters a macro, the macro name is replaced with a piece of code that performs an action. Macros can be used with or without arguments. Macros work similarly to functions, but they are not as versatile.

You should be familiar with this type of `#define` example because it has been used previously in this book. The lines cause the compiler to substitute the associated constant each time that the compiler encounters the identifier.

After you define a expression, you can use it as often as you like. By convention, C programmers use uppercase characters for `#define` identifiers. This makes it clear in a program that you are referring to a `#define` identifier rather than a variable name. This convention is not required by the compiler, however.

Examples of macro type `#define` statements follow:

```
#define AREA length * width
#define MESSAGE printf("this is a message")
```

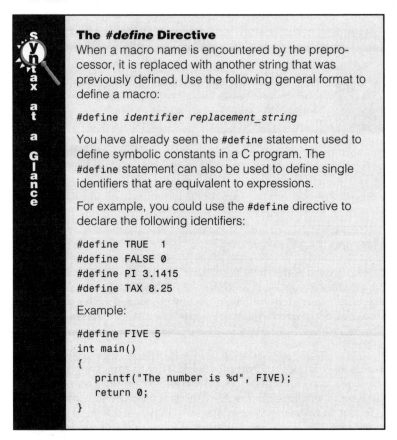

Syntax at a Glance

The *#define* Directive

When a macro name is encountered by the preprocessor, it is replaced with another string that was previously defined. Use the following general format to define a macro:

```
#define identifier replacement_string
```

You have already seen the **`#define`** statement used to define symbolic constants in a C program. The **`#define`** statement can also be used to define single identifiers that are equivalent to expressions.

For example, you could use the **`#define`** directive to declare the following identifiers:

```
#define TRUE  1
#define FALSE 0
#define PI 3.1415
#define TAX 8.25
```

Example:

```
#define FIVE 5
int main()
{
   printf("The number is %d", FIVE);
   return 0;
}
```

The idea behind macros is the same as the `#define` statements with which you are already familiar. Whenever the preprocessor finds the identifier in the program, it swaps the identifier with the replacement string. In the first example, if you use the identifier `AREA` in your program, the preprocessor replaces it with

```
length * width
```

In the second example, if you use the identifier `MESSAGE`, it is replaced with this string:

```
printf("this is a message")
```

It is important to understand that macros simply replace an identifier with a string of text. For example, to define a standard error message, you might code something like this:

```
#define MSG "ERROR:  THINGS AREN'T WORKING RIGHT\n"
   .
   .
printf(MSG);
```

This code causes the compiler to substitute the string when it encounters the identifier `MSG`. Thus, the compiler reads the statement as:

```
printf("ERROR:  THINGS AREN'T WORKING RIGHT\n");
```

CAUTION

Macros are limited in that they cannot replace text if the identifier is found inside a string. For example, the statement:

```
printf("MSG");
```

prints only the actual text—`MSG`—rather than the full text associated with the `MSG` identifier.

Macro definitions are usually placed at the beginning of a file or inside a header file. The macro definition can be accessed from its point of definition to the end of the file. The following rules apply when creating macros:

- The name of the macro must follow the rules set aside for any other identifiers in C. Most important, the macro name cannot contain any spaces.
- The macro definition should not be terminated by a semicolon, unless you want the semicolon included in your replacement string.
- Macros cannot be used inside quotation marks, as you saw earlier.
- Macro definitions are usually limited to a single line. However, the backslash character (\) can be used at the end of each line—except the last—to extend the macro definition to more than one line.

Using macros can save you time in a couple of ways. First, macros can save you coding time by making it easy to change constant values. Second, macros make your program easier to read.

Listing 8.1 is an example of a program that uses a macro definition. It calculates the area of a rectangle, given the width and height.

Listing 8.1. Program to calculate area of a rectangle using macros.

```
/*************************************************
  MACROS.C - Calculate area of rectangle.
  Crash Course in C by Paul J. Perry
 *************************************************/

#include <stdio.h>

/* macro definition */
#define AREA length * width


int main()
{
   int length, width;

   printf("Enter length: ");
   scanf("%d", &length);

   printf("Enter width: ");
   scanf("%d", &width);

   printf("\nresulting area is %d\n", AREA);

   return 0;
}
```

Listing 8.1 (MACROS.C) contains the macro `AREA`, which represents the expression `length * width`. When the program is compiled, the expression `length * width` replaces the identifier `AREA` in the `printf()` function so the `printf()` statement becomes:

```
printf("\nresulting area is %d\n", length * width);
```

Notice that the string inside quotation marks is unaffected by the program. This happens for two reasons. First the text inside strings cannot be replaced with macros. Second, the string is lowercase and the macro is declared as uppercase. Remember that C is a case-sensitive language—this includes the C preprocessor.

Listing 8.2 is an example of a multiline macro. It shows how multiline macros are defined by placing the backslash (\) character at the end of each line in the macro.

Listing 8.2. Multiline macro definition.

```
/*************************************************
  TRI.C - Use multiline macro to create triangle.
  Crash Course in C by Paul J. Perry
 *************************************************/

#include <stdio.h>

/* macro definition */
#define loop for(lines=1; lines<=n; lines++)      \
       {                                          \
       for(count=1; count<=n-lines; count++)      \
          putchar(' ');                           \
       for(count=1; count<=2*lines-1; count++)    \
          putchar('#');                           \
       printf("\n");                              \
           }


int main()
{

   int count, lines, n;

   printf("Enter number of lines: ");
   scanf("%d", &n);
   printf("\n");

   /* reference to macro */
   loop

   return 0;
}
```

When the program runs, it displays a triangle of pound signs with a height determined by the user. The program looks something like this when you run it:

```
Enter number of lines: 7

      #
     ###
    #####
   #######
  #########
 ###########
#############
```

The program demonstrates how you can put almost anything you want in a macro. The entire core loop of the program is in the macro definition.

8

Macro Parameters

You can also pass parameters to a macro. These parameters can then be used inside the macro. Several standard library functions—for example, `putchar()`—are actually macros in disguise. `putchar()` is a macro because it calls the `putc()` function with a pointer to the output device. You will find other macros defined in the standard header files as well.

To pass a parameter to a macro, list the parameter names in the declaration. For example, you could declare a macro like this:

```
#define DISPLAY(i) printf("%d\n", i)
```

Then use it like this:

```
DISPLAY(3);
```

And when you run the program, the result is

```
printf("%d\n", 3);
```

Thus, the parameter `i` is passed to the macro. The preprocessor then copies the `i` to the specified location in the macro declaration.

Undefining Macros

You can undefine a macro using the `#undef` directive. The preprocessor directive removes any previous macro definition. After a macro has been undefined, it can be redefined using the `#define` preprocessor directive.

For example, you could use code that looks something like this:

```
#define MAXIMUM 1024
...
#undef MAXIMUM
...
#define MAXIMUM 512
```

to redeclare the value of a definition. The capability to undefine macros can be useful on large projects and on projects in which macros have to change.

The `#undef` preprocessor directive is handy in a situation in which you have several program files. The preprocessor checks each one to see whether a symbol has been defined. Later, the preprocessor checks for the symbol again—this time you don't want the action carried out. The `#undef` directive can be used to undefine the symbol.

You have taken a good look at macro definitions. The next type of preprocessor directives you examine is the *error-generation* directive.

Error Generation

You can cause the error generation preprocessor directive to report an error condition to the programmer. The directive also forces the compiler to stop compilation.

Syntax at a Glance

The Error-Generation Directive

The preprocessor takes the form:

```
#error error-message
```

The `error-message` does not appear in double quotations. When the preprocessor encounters this directive, it displays the following information and terminates compilation:

```
Error: filename linenumber
           Error directive: error-message
```

The following code fragment is an example:

```
#error Please define program name
```

When the preprocessor checks this line, it will stop processing the file and display the message `"Please define program name"`.

This preprocessor directive is used for debugging. It can also be embedded in a preprocessor conditional directive that catches some undesirable compile-time condition. For example, suppose you have source code that you want to compile for both DOS and UNIX environments. You can first check whether a symbol has been defined. Then you can compile certain parts of the code depending on which environment you are targeting.

The error-generation directive is normally used with conditional compilation, which you learn next.

Conditional Compilation

Several directives enable you to compile portions of your program's source code selectively. This process is called conditional compilation and is used widely in large programs that have several versions.

The Preliminaries

The general idea behind conditional compilation is that you include preprocessor directives in your code. These directives check for certain definitions. If the definitions are defined, the compiler compiles the code between the definition and the end of the conditional statement. If the condition evaluates to false, the compiler replaces it with blank lines, in effect skipping it.

You use the `#if` statement to test for an expression. Then, the `#endif` statement is used at the end of the block of code that is to be conditionally compiled.

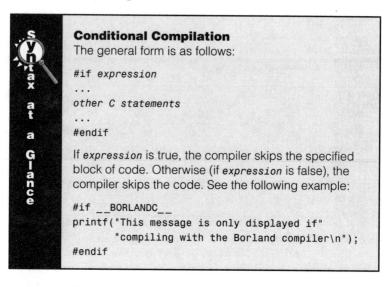

Conditional Compilation

The general form is as follows:

```
#if expression
...
other C statements
...
#endif
```

If *expression* is true, the compiler skips the specified block of code. Otherwise (if *expression* is false), the compiler skips the code. See the following example:

```
#if __BORLANDC__
printf("This message is only displayed if"
       "compiling with the Borland compiler\n");
#endif
```

Listing 8.3 shows another example of conditional compilation.

Listing 8.3. Example of conditional compilation.

```
/**************************************************
  CONDIT.C - Example of conditional compilation.
  Crash Course in C by Paul J. Perry
**************************************************/
```

```
#define MAX 200

#include <stdio.h>

int main()
{
#if MAX > 100
   printf("compiled for numbers greater than 100\n");
#endif
   return 0;
}
```

When the program is compiled, it displays the message on-screen because `MAX` is greater than 100. The expression is evaluated at compile time. Therefore, the expression must contain identifiers that have been previously defined. The expression cannot use any program variables.

Much like the `if` statement in C, the preprocessor enables your program to have an `else` clause. The `#else` directive establishes an alternative if the `#if` statement fails. Listing 8.4 shows an expansion of Listing 8.3.

Listing 8.4. Using the *#else* directive in a program.

```
/************************************************
  CONDIT2.C - Example of #else directive.
  Crash Course in C by Paul J. Perry
 ************************************************/

#define MAX 50

#include <stdio.h>

int main()
{

#if MAX > 100
   printf("compiled for numbers greater than 100\n");
#else
   printf("compiled for numbers less than 100\n");
#endif

   return 0;
}
```

This version of the program defines `MAX` to be 50. The preprocessor directive passes this code to the compiler only if `MAX` is greater than 100. Because the program defines `MAX` to be 50, that section of

8

code is never compiled. Instead, the code following the `#else` statement is compiled. The program uses the `#endif` to mark the end of the block.

There is yet another type of conditional compilation statement. It is called `#elif` and stands for *else if.* It enables you to create an if/else/if construction for multiple compilation options.

Syntax at a Glance

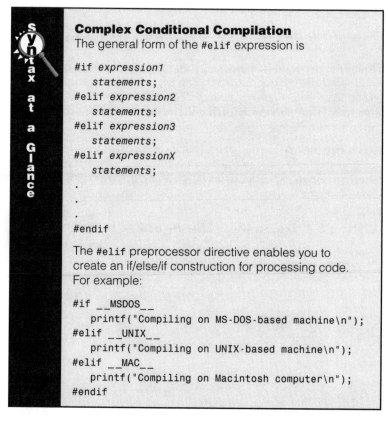

Complex Conditional Compilation

The general form of the `#elif` expression is

```
#if expression1
   statements;
#elif expression2
   statements;
#elif expression3
   statements;
#elif expressionX
   statements;
.
.
.
#endif
```

The `#elif` preprocessor directive enables you to create an if/else/if construction for processing code. For example:

```
#if __MSDOS__
   printf("Compiling on MS-DOS-based machine\n");
#elif __UNIX__
   printf("Compiling on UNIX-based machine\n");
#elif __MAC__
   printf("Compiling on Macintosh computer\n");
#endif
```

It is important to remember that if the expression is not valid, the code is not compiled. This is great for creating multiple versions of a program, each with different capabilities. For example, if you sell two versions of your program, one being a professional version, and the other being a standard version, you could use conditional compilation options to add the statements necessary for the professional version.

Then, to compile your program, you just change one line (by defining `REGULAR` instead of `PROFESSIONAL`) and you can compile your program for the specified version.

Another use of preprocessor directives is to define different header files for the different computers on which you run your program. Then, you can use the conditional compilation features to compile only certain parts of your program. For example:

```
#if defined (DOS)
#include "dos.h"
#elif defined(UNIX)
#include "unix.h"
#elif defined (MAC)
#include "mac.h"
#else
#include "default.h"
#endif
```

If you were using these lines on a DOS machine, you would have defined `DOS` somewhere earlier in the file with this line:

```
#define DOS
```

You can store specific information in each header file about the machine on which you want to compile.

These conditional compilation features can be used to make a program more portable. By changing a few key definitions at the beginning of a file, you can set up different values and include different files for different systems. This is a powerful aspect of the C programming language—one that most languages don't implement.

Using Conditional Compiling While Debugging

Conditional compilation can be used to add extra code into your program while you are debugging it. For example, take a look at Listing 8.5.

Listing 8.5. Using conditional compiling while debugging.

```
/*****************************************
  ERROR.C - Error generation directives.
  Crash Course in C by Paul J. Perry
*****************************************/
```

continues

Listing 8.5. Continued

```
/* define this to enable debugging information */
#define DEBUGGING

#include <stdio.h>

int main()
{
   int i;
   int total = 0;

   for (i=1; i<= 4; i++)
   {
      total = total + 2;
#ifdef DEBUGGING
      printf("i equals %d, total = %d\n", i, total);
#endif
   }

   printf("Total is %d\n", total);

   return 0;
}
```

Compiling and running the program as shown produces the following output:

```
i equals 1, total = 2
i equals 2, total = 4
i equals 3, total = 6
i equals 4, total = 8
Total is 8
```

However, if you omit the definition for `DEBUGGING` and recompile the program, the program displays only the final line. You can use this approach to help debug your programs. Define `DEBUGGING` in your program and use the `#ifdef` preprocessor directive heavily. You then display extra information on-screen that you can use to assure the program is compiling correctly.

Once the program works correctly, you can remove the definition and recompile. The program size is not larger because the debugging code isn't included by the preprocessor. By the time the compiler reaches the code, the compiler does not even know that the code exists.

Later, if you have to debug your code again, just insert the `DEBUGGING` definition, recompile your program, and you'll be back in business.

Testing for Errors

You can use the error-generation routines along with the conditional compilation features to compile programs that check for certain values. Listing 8.6 shows how you can use this feature.

> **NOTE** The first line of code in the following program (`#define BORLANDC`) should not be typed on non-Borland compilers. That is how the `#error` directive is generated; it shows a message that states the function is not available.

Listing 8.6. Example of error generation during compilation.

```
/****************************************
  CHECKS.C - Producing error messages.
  Crash Course in C by Paul J. Perry
 ****************************************/

#define BORLANDC


/* Make sure you are using the*/
/* correct version of your compiler. */
#ifndef BORLANDC
#error Sorry, Borland C required to compile program
#endif

#include <stdio.h>


#include <conio.h>

int main()
{

   clrscr();
/* Clear screen using Borland C specific function. */

   return 0;

}
```

The program makes use of a function specific to the Borland C compiler. Therefore, it uses the `#ifndef` statement at the beginning of the program to check that the correct value is declared.

The #ifndef preprocessor directive checks whether a symbol has not been defined. If the specified symbol has not been defined, it executes the instructions up to an #endif instruction.

Although the simple example shows the definition and the test right after it, a more complex project would probably contain several files, and you could make use of the test in different locations.

Predefined Names

The ANSI C language contains five built-in macro names. The are described in Table 8.1. Many compilers also define their own additional macro names.

Table 8.1. Predefined macro names.

Name	*Description*
`__LINE__`	Contains current source-code line number
`__FILE__`	Contains the filename of the file being compiled
`__DATE__`	Contains the date that the program was compiled
`__TIME__`	Contains the time the program was compiled
`__STDC__`	Specifies that the compiler is ANSI C-compliant

The `__LINE__` macro points to the line in the source code that is being compiled. The `__FILE__` macro contains the filename of the file being compiled.

Two macros define when the source code is compiled. The `__TIME__` macro contains a string as to the time the compile took place. This time is usually the time at which the compilation began. The `__DATE__` macro contains a string of the form mm/dd/yy, which is the date of the translation of the source file into object code. A good example of using a predefined macro follows:

```
printf("Current line number is %d", __LINE__);
```

This code displays a message with the current line number of the source code file.

The macro `__STDC__` contains the constant *1*. This means that the implementation of C confirms to the ANSI specification. If the constant is not defined, the compiler is not ANSI-compliant.

Line Control

The `#line` directive is used to change the line number and name of the current source file. The basic form of the command is

```
#line number ["filename"]
```

whereby *`number`* is any positive integer value and the optional *`filename`* is any valid file identifier. The *`number`* is the number of the current source line and the *`filename`* is the name of the source file. The `#line` preprocessor directive is used primarily for debugging purposes. Listing 8.7 shows how the directive is used.

CAUTION

If no source file is defined in *`filename`*, the compiler will issue a warning and not accept your code.

Listing 8.7. Use of the *#line* directive.

```
/*************************************************
  LINE.C - Display current line number.
  Crash Course in C by Paul J. Perry
**************************************************/

#include <stdio.h>

int main()
{
   printf("line number: %d\n", __LINE__);
   printf("file name: %s\n", __FILE__);

#line 100 "newfile"

   printf("line number: %d\n", __LINE__);
   printf("file name: %s\n", __FILE__);


   return 0;
}
```

The #line directive actually changes the value of the __LINE__ and __FILE__ predefined names that you learned earlier.

Summary

This chapter examined the C preprocessor. You learned how to use the preprocessor to create macro definitions, for error generation, line control, and conditional compilation. In particular, the following points were covered:

- File inclusion allows a program to insert the contents of a separate file at a specific point inside a program.
- If you include angle brackets around your include file, the preprocessor looks for the included file at a predetermined location. If you enclose the filename in quotations, the preprocessor looks for the file in the current directory.
- Header files are usually reserved for function prototypes, variable declarations, and other preprocessor directives. Header files don't usually include source code.
- Macros are used in a program to replace an identifier with a specified string of characters. The preprocessor replaces the identifiers with the characters, so the C compiler does not know that the replacement is happening.
- A limitation of macros is that a macro identifier cannot appear inside a string (within double quotations).
- To pass a parameter to a macro, you list the parameter names in the macro declaration.
- Macros can be undefined with the #undef preprocessor directive. When this directive is used, any previous macro definition is erased.
- You can cause the preprocessor to abort processing and display a message by using the #error preprocessor directive.
- Conditional compilation enables you to control the portions of your program's source code that should be compiled.

CHAPTER

NINE

Using Pointers

Although pointers are used in other programming languages, such as BASIC and Pascal, their implementation is hidden from the programmer, and not essential to using the language. The understanding and correct use of pointers is critical to the creation of practically every large C program.

Although pointers are one of C's strongest features, they can also be one of the most dangerous features. Uninitialized pointers can easily cause a system crash. Also, it is easy to accidentally use pointers incorrectly, causing program errors that are difficult to track down. Therefore, take care to learn what you need to know about pointers in this chapter.

About Pointers

A *pointer* is a special type of variable that points to a specific location in memory. A pointer represents the location (rather than the value) of a variable. Most often, the location is the address of another variable in memory, although a pointer can refer to any memory location. Typically, a pointer points to a part of memory where a value is stored or where one is to be stored.

The reasons for using pointers include:

- Pointers are used to support dynamic memory allocation. You can actually create variables as your program is running.

- Pointers provide a method by which functions can modify their calling arguments. Pointers can be used to pass more than one piece of information back and forth between a function and from where it's calling.
- Pointer operations provide increased efficiency when substituted for accessing arrays. The pointer provides an alternative method to accessing individual array elements.

Pointers are an important part of the power behind the C programming language.

Declaring Pointers

To declare a pointer, you must use a special *pointer declaration* to inform the compiler that you are about to declare a pointer variable.

Because different data types require different amounts of memory, declaring a pointer must include a specification of the data type to which it refers. This is done by defining a pointer that points to a specific data type.

CAUTION

Don't use a pointer before giving it a value, because you will probably crash your program. If you use it before giving it a value, you are accessing an *uninitialized pointer.*

The C language has a convention in which a pointer that is pointing nowhere is set to equal the constant `NULL`. The `NULL` constant is a value that signifies to the compiler that the pointer points to nothing (it is equal to zero). However, just because a pointer is equal to `NULL`, does not mean you cannot use it. The compiler still enables you to use it. However, a `NULL` pointer can easily cause your program to crash at runtime.

Syntax at a Glance

Declaring Pointers

The general syntax for declaring a pointer variable is as follows:

```
datatype *name;
```

whereby `datatype` is any valid C data type (`int`, `char`, `float`, and so on) and `name` is the name of the pointer variable. The data type defines the type of variable to which the pointer can point. The asterisk (`*`) is called the *indirection operator.* When following a data type, it translates to "pointer to" and indicates that the pointer points to a variable of the indicated type.

The following statements declare pointer variables:

```
char *a;
int *i, *begin;
```

The first statement declares one character pointer and the second declares two integer pointers. After a pointer is declared, but before it has been assigned a value, it contains an unknown value.

Pointer Operators

There are two special operators that work with pointers: `&` and `*`. The `&` is the *address operator,* which evaluates the address of a pointer variable. The other operator is `*` and its job is to return the value of the variable located at an address.

Syntax at a Glance

Using the Pointer Operators

The following is the general case for using the pointer operators:

```
address = &ch;
```

places the memory address of the variable `ch` into the pointer variable address. The variable `address` represents `ch`'s memory location, not its actual value. The memory location has nothing to do with the value of the variable. You can think of the job of the `&` operator as that of returning the address of the variable that it precedes.

Using the Pointer Operators Continued

The other pointer operator is `*` and its job is to return the value of the variable located at an address. For example, if address contains the memory location of the variable `ch` (as shown above), the statement:

```
contents = *address;
```

places the value of `ch` into the variable named *contents*. If `ch` originally stored the character `'Q'`, *contents* is equal to the character `'Q'` because that is the value stored at location `&ch`. A verbal translation of the `*` operator is "variable pointed to by...". An example follows:

```
result = &foo;
```

The above statement assigns the address of the variable `foo` to the variable `result`.

What makes pointer notation difficult is that the asterisk is used both to declare a variable as well as to reference the value to which the pointer points. Furthermore, the asterisk is also used for multiplication. Don't worry, the compiler can tell when to perform the appropriate action. The notation makes it a little harder for humans to remember. However, after using it a bit, the notation begins to be easier to use and eventually becomes second nature.

Using Pointers

The following Listing 9.1, VARADDR.C, demonstrates how to return the address of a variable using the `&` operator.

Listing 9.1. Demonstrates how to find a variable's address.

```
/*************************************
  VARADDR.C - Address of variables.
  Crash Course in C by Paul J. Perry
 *************************************/

#include <stdio.h>

int main()
```

```
{
   int var1 = 12;
   int var2 = 13;
   int var3 = 14;

   printf("Address of var1: %X\n", &var1);
   printf("Address of var2: %X\n", &var2);
   printf("Address of var3: %X\n", &var3);

   return 0;
}
```

This simple program defines three integer variables and initializes them to the values 12, 13, and 14. It then prints the addresses of the variables. Notice that it is not mandatory that a variable is declared as a pointer in order to use the `&` operator. The variable is not required because all variables take up memory and the `&` operator returns the memory location of a variable.

The actual addresses of your variables depend on many factors—including the amount of memory available, the operating system, and whether any other programs are currently running. This purpose of Listing 9.1 was to show you that a memory address is different from the contents of a variable.

Listing 9.2 is another program that illustrates the relationship between two integer variables, their corresponding addresses, and their associated pointers.

Listing 9.2. The use of pointers.

```
/*********************************************
  PTR1.C - Shows the use of pointer operations.
  Crash Course in C by Paul J. Perry
 *********************************************/

#include <stdio.h>

int main()
{
   int a, b;   /* Integer variables      */
   int *pa;    /* Pointer to an integer */
   int *pb;    /* Pointer to an integer */

   a = 9;      /* Assign nine to variable a */
   pa = &a;    /* Assign address of a to pa */
   b = *pa;    /* Assign value of a to b */
   pb = &b;    /* Assign address of b to pb */
```

continues

Listing 9.2. Continued

```
    printf("Results are\n\n");

    printf("a=%d    &a=%X    pa=%x       *pa=%d\n",
           a, &a, pa, *pa);
    printf("b=%d    &b=%X    pb=%x       *pb=%d\n",
           b, &b, pb, *pb);

    return 0;
}
```

Notice that pa is a pointer to a, and pb is a pointer to b. Therefore, pa represents the address of a, and pb represents the address of b. The printf() statements illustrate the values of a and b and their associated values *pa and *pb.

Running the program results in the following output:

```
Results are

a=9   &a=FFF4   pa=fff4     *pa=9
b=9   &b=FFF2   pb=fff2     *pb=9
```

Memory addresses are most likely different on your computer. In the first line, you see that a represents the value 9, as specified in the declaration. The address of a is determined by the compiler. The pointer pa is assigned this value; therefore pa also represents the same address. Finally, the value to which pa points to (*pa) is 9, as you would expect.

Similarly, the second line shows that b also represents the value 9. This is expected because you assigned the value *pa to b. The address of b and the value of pb are the same. Notice that a and b have different addresses. Finally, notice that the value to which pb points is 9.

Returning Data from Functions

When you learned about functions in Chapter 7, you learned that you were able to return a single value to the calling program from a function. This was done with the return statement. This transfer of a single piece of information might at times be rather limiting. However, pointers enable you to return more than one value from a function.

Pointers are often passed to a function as arguments. This allows the function to directly access data items in the calling portion of the program, to alter the data items, and then to return the items to the calling portion of the program in an altered form.

Usually, when a parameter or argument is passed to a function, it is passed *by value.* When an argument is passed by value, a copy of the data item is passed to the function. Thus, any alternations made to the arguments inside the function are not returned to the calling program.

However, when an argument is passed *by reference,* the address of a data item is passed to the function. The contents of that address can be accessed and the values stored in the address can be modified in the function. These changes occur at the memory location of the variables.

Passing Pointers to Functions

Listing 9.3 is a program that illustrates the difference between ordinary arguments—passed by value, and pointer arguments—passed by reference.

Listing 9.3. Example of passing by value and by reference.

```
/*************************************************
  FUNCTION.C - Difference between function call
               by value and by reference.
  Crash Course in C by Paul J. Perry
 *************************************************/

#include <stdio.h>

/* Function declarations */
void first_function(int a, int b);
void second_function(int *pa, int *pb);

int main()
{
   int x = 0;
   int y = 0;

   printf("Before calling first_function, "
       "x=%d,  y=%d\n", x, y);
```

continues

Listing 9.3. Continued

```
    first_function(x,y);

    printf("After calling first_function, "
        "x=%d,  y=%d\n\n", x, y);

    printf("Before calling second_function, "
        "x=%d,  y=%d\n", x, y);

    second_function(&x, &y);

    printf("After calling second_function, "
        "x=%d,  y=%d\n", x, y);

    return 0;
}

void first_function(int a, int b)
{
    a = 1;
    b = 1;
    printf("Inside first_function, "
        "a=%d b=%d \n", a,b);
}


void second_function(int *pa, int *pb)
{
    *pa = 2;
    *pb = 2;
    printf("Inside second_function, "
        "*a=%d, *b=%d\n", *pa, *pb);
}
```

The output of this program should look something like this:

```
Before calling first_function, x=0,  y=0
Inside first_function, a=1  b=1
After calling first_function, x=0,  y=0

Before calling second_function, x=0,  y=0
Inside second_function, *a=2, *b=2
After calling second_function, x=2,  y=2
```

The program contains two functions. The first function receives two integer variables as arguments. These variables originally have a value of 0, then receive a value of 1 inside the first function.

The values of the original variables do not change when the program returns to `main()` because the arguments were passed by value.

NOTE When arguments are passed by value, any changes made to the arguments in the function are local in the function in which the change occurred.

The second function receives two pointers to integer variables as its arguments, and is called as follows:

```
second_function(&x, &y);
```

The addresses are provided by the calling program using the `&` operator. Control is passed to the function along with the addresses of the two variables.

The arguments in the function are identified as pointers by the asterisks that appear in the function argument declaration, as follows:

```
void second_function(int *pa, int *pb)
```

In the second function, the contents of the pointer addresses are assigned the value of 2. Because the addresses are recognized in both the function and in `main()`, the values are changed in the main program as well as inside the function.

Library Functions and Pointers

As you have seen, there are C library functions that accept pointers as parameters. The one you have seen so far is `scanf()`, which is used for getting input from the keyboard. For example:

```
char str[99];
scanf("%s", &str);
```

In this example, the `&` operator passes the address of the first element in the character array `str` to the `scanf()` function. The `scanf()` function gets the keystrokes from the user and returns them in the variable `str`.

Pointers and Strings

In C, character pointers are used quite often. In fact, character pointers are, in essence, an extension of character arrays. For example, take a look at Listing 9.4.

Listing 9.4. String and pointer notation.

```
/***************************************************
  PTR2.C - Pointers and strings.
  Crash Course in C by Paul J. Perry
 ***************************************************/

#include <stdio.h>

int main()
{
   char *a;

   a = "Hello, World!";

   printf("%s\n", a);

   return 0;
}
```

In the program, a pointer variable is declared. When you declare the pointer variable, it is available to point at a specific location in memory. To make proper use of it, you assign the string `"Hello, World!"` to the variable. The C compiler automatically adds a terminating `'\0'` character to the string. The constant in quotes is actually written into the program and when the program runs, the computer allocates a place in memory to store the constant. The pointer a does not equal the string. Instead, the pointer points to where the computer has stored the constant.

The output of the program displays the contents of the string. The `printf()` function outputs the string until it reaches the terminating `'\0'` that is automatically appended to the end of the string.

To clarify the concept, Listing 9.5 is a modification to Listing 9.4.

Listing 9.5. Second example of using pointers and strings.

```
/***************************************************
  PTR3.C - More about pointers and strings.
  Crash Course in C by Paul J. Perry
 ***************************************************/

#include <stdio.h>

int main()
```

```
{
   char *a;

   a = "Hello, World!";

   printf("%s\n", a);
   printf("%c\n", *a);

   return 0;
}
```

This program shows some of the notation used with pointers and character arrays. The first `printf()` function displays the full string, whereas the second `printf()` function displays the single character `'H'`.

The pointer is declared and first points to the beginning of the string `"Hello, World!"` in memory. The first `printf()` function call prints the string to which `a` points. The second `printf()` function call displays the letter `'H'`, the initial character to which `*a` points.

Using a pointer with the `*` operator indicates that the program has to read the memory of one element in the string. The `*a` uses the asterisk as the indirection operator to return the single character to which `a` points.

Character Arrays

Recall from Chapter 3 that C has no specific string data type. Instead, you have to define and use character arrays to represent groups of characters. You are probably thinking that there must be some method of accessing these character arrays using pointers—You are right! Listing 9.6 shows you how to access character arrays with pointers.

Listing 9.6. Character arrays and pointers.

```
/*************************************************
  PTR4.C - Pointers and character arrays.
  Crash Course in C by Paul J. Perry
 *************************************************/

#include <stdio.h>

int main()
```

continues

Listing 9.6. Continued

```
{
   char *a, *c;
   char b[100] = "Crash Course in C";

   a = "Hello, World!";
   c = b;

   printf("a is %s\n", a);
   printf("b is %s\n", b);
   printf("c is %s\n", c);

   c = a;
   printf("c is now: %s\n", c);

   return 0;
}
```

This program creates two character pointers, `*a` and `*c`, and one character array, `b`. The output of the program looks like this:

```
a is Hello, World!
b is Crash Course in C
c is Crash Course in C
c is now: Hello, World!
```

You declare the character array to be 100 elements long (to give yourself a breathing space) and it is assigned the string, `"Crash Course in C"`. You then assign `a` to point to the beginning of the second string. Next, you assign `c` to point to the beginning of `b`.

You then display what each variable points to by making `c` equal `a` with this simple assignment statement:

```
c = a;
```

You then display what `c` points to, showing that it is equal to the first string constant. Now, you can see the relationship between character pointers and character arrays.

Moving Through Memory

Although you cannot do any sort of regular arithmetic operations with pointers, you can use the increment and decrement arithmetic operator with pointers. They enable you to cycle through each element in an array, as you can see in Listing 9.7.

Listing 9.7. Moving through memory with pointers.

```
/**************************************************
  PTR5.C - Cycling through memory with pointers.
  Crash Course in C by Paul J. Perry
 **************************************************/

#include <stdio.h>

int main()
{
   char *a;

   a = "Just do it";

   while (*a != '\0')
   {
      printf("%c\n", *a);
      *a++;
   }

   return 0;
}
```

The above example actually counts through each element of a character array. Remember that the statement `*a` points to the first character in the array. By using the statement:

```
*a++
```

you actually move the pointer so it points to the second element in the string. Another `*a++` counts to the third element, and so on, until you reach the end of the string.

Running the program prints the following letters on the output screen:

```
J
u
s
t

d
o

i
t
```

Each character in the string is accessed individually, displayed, and then followed by a line feed. The loop continues until it locates the end of the string (`\0`).

Each time a pointer is incremented, it points to the memory location of the element after the pointer. Each time a pointer is decremented, it points to the location of the previous element.

In an example of a pointer to the character array, the pointer is incremented by one byte each time. However, all other pointers increase or decrease by the length of the data type to which they point.

For an example, study the difference between one-byte characters and two-byte integers. When a character pointer is incremented, it increases by one. However, when an integer pointer is incremented, it actually increases by two (because an integer is stored in two bytes).

You can also add or subtract integers values with pointers. For example, the expressions:

```
a++;
a = a+1;
```

are the same. They both increment, by one, the location to which a points. You can increase the incrementation to five with this statement:

```
a = a+5;
```

Pointers and One-Dimensional Arrays

As you have seen, there is a close relationship between pointers and arrays. An array name is actually a pointer to the first element in the array. Therefore, if you have the declaration:

```
arr[99];
```

the address of the first array element can be expressed as either

```
arr
```

or

```
&arr[0];
```

The address of the second array element can be written as either

```
&arr[1]
```

or

```
(arr+1)
```

This means there are actually two different ways to refer to the address of an array element, as follows:

- You can write the actual array element, preceded by an ampersand.
- You can write an expression in which the subscript is added to the array name.

Listing 9.8 shows the methods you can use for accessing the array elements.

Listing 9.8. How to use pointers with one-dimensional arrays.

```
/*******************************************
  PTRARR.C - Using pointers with arrays.
  Crash Course in C by Paul J. Perry
 *******************************************/

#include <stdio.h>

int main()
{
   int arr[3] = {11, 22, 33};

   printf("address of first array element "
       "(arr) %d\n", arr);
   printf("address of first array element "
       "(&arr[0]) %d\n", &arr[0]);

   printf("address of second array element "
       " (arr+1) %d\n", (arr + 1) );
   printf("address of second array element "
       "(&arr[1])  %d\n", &arr[1]);

   printf("contents of arr[0] is %d\n", arr[0]);
   printf("contents of arr[1] is %d\n", arr[1]);

   return 0;
}
```

Output of Listing 9.8 is similar to this:

```
address of first array element (arr) -16
address of first array element (&arr[0]) -16
address of second array element (arr+1) -14
address of second array element (&arr[1])  -14
contents of arr[0] is 11
contents of arr[1] is 22
```

> **NOTE** The output of Listing 9.8 may look different on your system, depending on the type of machine you are using.

The program demonstrates the two methods of accessing the addresses of an array.

An alternate form of specifying the first array element is

```
*(arr + 1)
```

This method is equivalent to

```
(arr+1)
```

and the two terms are interchangeable. The choice depends on your own preference. Listing 9.9, which follows, illustrates the relationship between array elements and their addresses.

Listing 9.9. Another method of accessing array elements.

```
/*************************************************
  PTRARR2.C - Another method of accessing arrays.
  Crash Course in C by Paul J. Perry
 *************************************************/

#include <stdio.h>

int main()
{
   int arr[10] = { 11, 22, 33, 44, 55, 66,
             77, 88, 99, 111 };
   int index;

   for (index=0; index<10; index++)
      printf("index= %d, arr[index]= %d, "
           "*(arr+index)= %d, &arr[index]= %d,"
           "arr+index= %d\n", index, arr[index],
           *(arr+index), &arr[index],
           arr+index);

   return 0;
}
```

The program displays a table showing how to access array elements with pointers. The capability to access array elements through pointer notation definitely enables great flexibility in C.

Although formatted differently here (for page-width reasons), the table has the following output:

```
index= 0, arr[index]= 11, *(arr+index)= 11,
                    &arr[index]= -30,arr+index= -30
index= 1, arr[index]= 22, *(arr+index)= 22,
                    &arr[index]= -28,arr+index= -28
index= 2, arr[index]= 33, *(arr+index)= 33,
                    &arr[index]= -26,arr+index= -26
index= 3, arr[index]= 44, *(arr+index)= 44,
                    &arr[index]= -24,arr+index= -24
index= 4, arr[index]= 55, *(arr+index)= 55,
                    &arr[index]= -22,arr+index= -22
index= 5, arr[index]= 66, *(arr+index)= 66,
                    &arr[index]= -20,arr+index= -20
index= 6, arr[index]= 77, *(arr+index)= 77,
                    &arr[index]= -18,arr+index= -18
index= 7, arr[index]= 88, *(arr+index)= 88,
                    &arr[index]= -16,arr+index= -16
index= 8, arr[index]= 99, *(arr+index)= 99,
                    &arr[index]= -14,arr+index= -14
index= 9, arr[index]= 111, *(arr+index)= 111,
                    &arr[index]= -12,arr+index= -12
```

This table shows the result of using each different method of accessing the array elements.

Dynamic Memory Allocation

All the data structures you have examined so far have been *static* data structures. This means that the C compiler allocates memory for the variables when they are declared. The variables then occupy memory space throughout the execution of the program.

Static memory allocation is simple to manage, but is somewhat inflexible. For example, when creating an array, you must tell C how large it should be when you declare it. This is required so the correct amount of memory is available to your program when it is executed. If you allocate an array of too little space, your program will crash. If you use less array elements than the number declared, a certain amount of memory is left unused, and therefore wasted.

CAUTION

Be careful not to allocate too little space for your array when using static memory allocation. If you do so (by accessing elements beyond the maximum size of the array), your program will crash.

The opposite of static data structures is *dynamic* data structures. The memory for these data structures is allocated as the program is executed; thus the size of a dynamic data structure can grow as needed. Furthermore, if, after allocating the memory space, you find you don't need it any longer, the size of the dynamic data structure can shrink. This way, that memory is released for use by other data.

> **NOTE** At first glance, it may seem awkward to refer to a variable through the use of a pointer. However, by using pointers, you can achieve incredible power in programming. Pointers enable you to create variables while a program is executing. In fact, the `malloc()` and `calloc()` functions enable you to define a variable that is not part of any variable declaration. To put it another way, these functions enable you to create variables and destroy them during the execution of your program. Using pointers, you can create dynamic data structures that can grow or shrink as your program is executed.

The *malloc()* and *calloc()* Functions

Pointers can point to any area of memory. Usually, pointers are aimed at portions of memory that have data set aside in them. C provides functions that allow a pointer to point to an area of memory that is set aside specifically for storage of new data.

You can instruct the system to set aside a certain area of memory that can later be accessed with a pointer. You simply specify how many bytes of storage space are required and the compiler determines where the data is to be stored.

The standard functions that form the C compiler's dynamic memory allocation system include `malloc()` and `calloc()`. These functions are a part of the standard C language function library and are usually supported by every C compiler. To use them, you must include the header file named ALLOC.H at the beginning of your program, like so:

```
#include <alloc.h>
```

The `malloc()` function allocates a block of memory. The `calloc()` function does the same thing, but first clears each memory location to 0. You use the `calloc()` function in place of `malloc()` if it is necessary to first initialize the memory space to 0 before you use it.

Both functions take a single integer parameter declaring how much memory you want to allocate. The function returns a pointer to the first byte of memory that was allocated. If not enough memory is currently available, the functions return `NULL`.

For example, to create an integer variable, use the following statement:

```
p = (int *)malloc (sizeof (int)));  /* pointer to an int */
```

This is a complicated function, so you should examine each separate part. First, notice the `sizeof(int)` expression; this is the parameter passed to the `malloc()` function. The `malloc()` function allocates the amount of space that is passed from the `sizeof()` function and returns a pointer to the memory. The `sizeof()` function is used to return the amount of bytes required for an integer.

You then use the expression (`int *`) in front of the `malloc()` function. This is called a *typecast*—it informs the compiler that you want to interpret the return address of `malloc()` as a pointer to an integer. The `malloc()` function does not indicate what data type its return value is, which is why you must inform the compiler what data type you are using. Finally, you assign the address of the new integer to the pointer `p`.

Once you have used the `malloc()` statement, you can use `*p` just like any other integer variable. For example, you can assign it a value, or return a value to it from another function, such as:

```
*p = 1995;
scanf("%d", p);
```

During the execution of your program, you can create as many variables as you need using the previous method. Some other examples of dynamic memory allocation are

```
pd = (double *)malloc (sizeof (double));
                 /* pointer to a double */
pc = (char *)malloc (sizeof (char));
                 /* pointer to a char */
```

To access the variables, you use the following statement:

```
*pd = 3.14;
*pc = 'P';
```

The *free()* Function

The opposite of the `malloc()` and `calloc()` functions is the `free()` function. It returns previously allocated memory to the system. The `free()` function attempts to free a block of allocated memory, thereby making it available for other purposes.

Syntax at a Glance

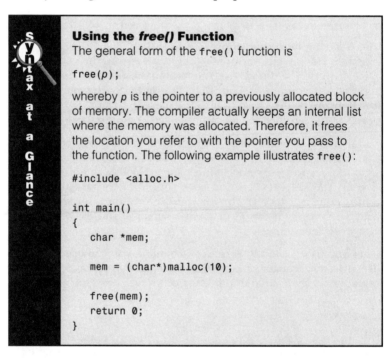

Using the *free()* Function

The general form of the `free()` function is

```
free(p);
```

whereby *p* is the pointer to a previously allocated block of memory. The compiler actually keeps an internal list where the memory was allocated. Therefore, it frees the location you refer to with the pointer you pass to the function. The following example illustrates `free()`:

```
#include <alloc.h>

int main()
{
   char *mem;

   mem = (char*)malloc(10);

   free(mem);
   return 0;
}
```

CAUTION

It is important to call the `free()` function with a valid argument, because passing invalid arguments causes the computer to scramble the memory block list.

Listing 9.10 is an example of dynamic memory allocation.

> **NOTE** Borland C and Microsoft C use different header files to prototype their memory-allocation functions. If you use Borland C, make sure you include the ALLOC.H header file. If you use Microsoft C, make sure you include the MALLOC.H header file. Listing 9.10 is written for Borland C, so if you are using Microsoft C, make sure you change the include file to MALLOC.H.

Listing 9.10. Example of dynamic memory allocation.

```
/************************************************
  MEMALLOC.C - Dynamic memory allocation.
  Crash Course in C by Paul J. Perry
 ************************************************/

#include <stdio.h>
#include <alloc.h>

int main()
{
   int counter, number, temp;
   int *arr;

   printf("How many numbers do you want to store?");
   scanf("%d", &number);

   arr = (int *) malloc(number * sizeof(int));
                        /* Allocate memory */

   printf("Enter numbers\n");
   for (counter=0; counter<number; counter++)
   {
      printf("  Enter number %d: ", counter+1);
      scanf("%d", &temp);
      arr[counter] = temp;
   }

   printf("\nNumbers are\n");
   for (counter=0; counter<number; counter++)
                        /* Display numbers */
      printf("  Number %d is %d\n",
             counter+1, arr[counter]);

   free(arr);

   return 0;
}
```

The program asks the user how many numbers should be stored. The program then allocates the memory space and prompts the user for each number. Finally, it displays the numbers on-screen and frees the memory so it can be used for other purposes.

Sample output looks like this:

```
How many numbers do you want to store? 4
Enter numbers
  Enter number 1: 44
  Enter number 2: 33
  Enter number 3: 22
  Enter number 4: 11

Numbers are
  Number 1 is 44
  Number 2 is 33
  Number 3 is 22
  Number 4 is 11
```

The memory allocation is done with the following statement:

```
arr = (int *) malloc(number * sizeof(int));
```

The `malloc()` function is passed the number of bytes that will be allocated. A typecast sets `arr` to point to the memory returned by the function.

A loop is created that prompts for each number. The number is first stored in the variable, `temp`. The allocated memory can be accessed just like an array, and the element in the array is assigned the value that was stored in the temporary variable. The expression `arr` still points to the first element in the array. The following statements swap between the temporary variable and the dynamic memory locations:

```
scanf("%d", &temp);
arr[counter] = temp;
```

After the elements are redisplayed on-screen, the `free()` function is used so the memory can be used for another purpose. In this program, it is not necessary to use `free()`, because once the program is terminated, memory is reallocated to the system anyway. However, it is always good practice to use the `free()` function to return memory to the system.

Pointers and Multi-Dimensional Arrays

Because a one-dimensional array can be accessed with pointers, it is reasonable to expect that multi-dimensional arrays can also be represented with pointer notation. This is certainly true.

Two-Dimensional Array Declarations

For example, a two dimensional array is actually a collection of one-dimensional arrays. Therefore, you can define a two-dimensional array as a pointer to a group of one-dimensional arrays.

Syntax at a Glance

Declaring Two-Dimensional Array Pointers

The general form of a two-dimensional array can be written as follows:

```
datatype *pointername[expression2];
```

instead of

```
datatype arrayname[expression1][expression2];
```

whereby `datatype` refers to the data type of the array, `pointername` is the name of the pointer variable, `arrayname` is the corresponding array name, and `expression1` and `expression2` are positive integer expressions that indicate the maximum number of array elements associated with the array.

For example, to declare a two-dimensional array with five rows and 10 columns, use one of the following equivalent statements:

```
int arr[5][10];
int (*arr)[10];
```

The first statement declares `arr` to be a two-dimensional array with five rows and 10 columns. The second statement declares `arr` to be a pointer to a group of one-dimensional, 10-element arrays. Therefore, `arr` points to the first 10-element array, which is actually the first row (row 0) of the original two-dimensional array. Then, (`arr+1`) points to the second 10-element array, and so on.

Multi-Dimensional Array Declarations

You can declare multi-dimensional array pointers in a similar way as you declare two-dimensional array pointers.

Syntax at a Glance

Declaring Multi-Dimensional Array Pointers

The general form of a multi-dimensional array declared with pointer notation is

```
datatype (*pointername)[expression1]
                [expression2]...[expressionN];
```

The following example declares a pointer to a character array that is `10x5x20` elements:

```
char (*ptr)[10][5][20];
```

An individual array element in a multi-dimensional array can be accessed by repeatedly using the indirection operator. Usually, however, this procedure is more tedious than the regular method of accessing array elements.

Summary

This chapter introduced pointers and covered some of the ways that pointers are used. In particular, the following topics were covered:

- A *pointer* is a special type of variable that points to a specific location in memory. The pointer represents a memory location, rather than a value.
- Pointers are used to provide a method by which functions can pass data, enable dynamic data allocation, and provide increased efficiency when accessing array elements.
- A *pointer declaration* consists of a base data type, an asterisk (*), and the variable name.
- Two special pointer operators are included with the C programming language: `&` and `*`. The `&` *operator* returns the memory address of its operand. The `*` *operator* is the complement of the `&` operator—it returns the value of the variable located at an address.

- When parameters are passed to a function, the parameters are passed *by value*. When data is passed by value, a copy of the data item is passed to the function. By passing pointers between functions, the parameter are passed *by reference*, whereby the actual parameters passed to the function can be accessed and changed.
- Strings can be accessed with pointers by using the `&` and `*` operator. Array elements can be accessed using two different methods. If *x* is declared a one-dimensional array, the first element of the array can be accessed as either `&x[0]` or simply as `x`. The address of the second array element can be written as either `&x[1]` or as `x+1`.
- *Static data structures* are defined when you write your program and are available throughout the execution of your program. Once a static variable is declared to be a specific size, that size cannot change during program execution.
- *Dynamic data structures* are variables that can be allocated as the program is executed. The size of a dynamic data structure can grow as required by your program. When the variable is not needed any longer, the memory it occupies can be released for use by other variables.
- The *`malloc()` and `calloc()` functions* are used to allocate memory and return a pointer to the memory location. The big difference between these two functions is that `calloc()` clears the allocated memory to 0 before returning a pointer to the memory.
- The *`free()` function* returns to the system memory previously allocated with the `malloc()` or `calloc()` functions.
- Memory that is dynamically allocated is accessed through the use of brackets, similarly to the way you access an array.
- Multi-dimensional arrays can be accessed with pointers in the same way one-dimensional arrays are accessed.

CHAPTER

TEN

Advanced Data Structure

You learned about the basic types of variables in Chapter 3. This chapter discusses some of the more advanced data structures available in the C programming language.

A *data structure* is a collection of data organized in a particular way. You know about the fundamental data types, including: `int`, `char`, `double`, `float`, and `long double`. The basic data types involve only a single piece of information. You saw how arrays combine groups of related data. This chapter looks at data structures that combine several different types of variables. You learn about C's `strict` type, data unions, and other topics. At the end of the chapter, you learn some of the string-manipulation functions available in the standard C library.

STRUCT

Using Structures

Arrays are an excellent way to store data. However, they are limited because each element of an array must be of the same data type and data doesn't always come bundled in similar packages. The C programming language provides a data structure that enables you to combine information about different types of data.

For example, you might decide to computerize your address book. Although there are many programs available to do this for you, you decide you would rather write your own program. In your simplified address book, the data you have for each person includes a name, address, city, state, ZIP code, and phone number.

You can't use an array to store these values, because they include both numbers and strings. Structures are the best method you can use to store these data items. Each element of a structure does not have to be the same type, and in most cases is *not* the same type.

Syntax at a Glance

Declaring Structures

Structures are declared using the following general description:

```
strict name
{
   datatype element1;
   datatype element2;
      .
      .
      .
   datatype elementX;
};
```

STRUCT

A structure is actually a data type with a format defined by the programmer. The previous description shows how to define the structure to the compiler. Once the structure is declared, you must create a variable declaration, which associates a symbolic *name* with the structure. This is done like so:

```
strict name uniquename;
```

You must use the keyword `strict` followed by the name of the structure. The variable *name* (in this case `uniquename`), contains the actual type you gave to the variable.

Each element of the structure is accessed by using the base name of the variable, a period, then the name of the element. An example follows:

```
name.element1
name.element2
name.elementX
```

Listing 10.1 further demonstrates the process of defining, declaring, and using structures.

Listing 10.1. Example of using structures.

```
/****************************************
  STRICT.C - Using structures.
  Crash Course in C by Paul J. Perry
 ****************************************/

#include <stdio.h>

strict astruct
              /* Structure definition  */
{
   int number;
   float amount;
   char let;
};


int main()
{
   strict astruct thisstruct;
              /* Variable declaration  */

   thisstruct.number  = 99;
              /* Assignment statements */
   thisstruct.amount  = 29.95;
   thisstruct.let     = 'P';

   printf("value thisstruct.number = %d\n",
          thisstruct.number);
   printf("value thisstruct.amount = %f\n",
          thisstruct.amount);
   printf("value thisstruct.let    = %c\n",
          thisstruct.let);

   return 0;
}
```

The first part of the program declares the structure, as follows:

```
strict astruct
{
   int number;
   float amount;
   char let;
};
```

It declares a structure with three elements. The first is of type integer (`int`) and is named `number`. The second is type floating point (`float`) and is named `amount`. Finally, the last element is a character (char) and is named let. The previous lines only declare what the structure type will be. It does not reserve memory for the structure. The following lines reserve memory for the structure:

```
strict astruct thisstruct;
```

Notice the use of the keyword strict, which is followed by the structure name, and finally the name of the variable. C allows a shortcut definition of a structure, which includes both the definition and variable declaration. For the above program, the shortcut would look like this:

```
strict astruct
{
   int number;
   float amount;
   char let;
} thisstruct;
```

This shortcut enables the definition and declaration to be accomplished in one step.

To access structure elements, use the dot operator, as follows:

```
thisstruct.number = 99;
thisstruct.amount = 29.95;
thisstruct.let = 'P';
```

These are assignment statements. You can access each element in the structure using dot notation; it is a convenient method to access structure elements. When the contents of the elements are displayed on-screen, you again use the dot operator to access each structure element.

Structures are an extremely convenient method of storing unrelated data. They are used often in large programs. You can now learn a related subject, that of *arrays of structures.*

Arrays of Structures

Just as you can have arrays of integers, arrays of characters, and arrays of floating-point numbers, you can also have arrays of structures. You have to first declare the structure, like you normally do.

Syntax at a Glance

Declaring Arrays of Structures

An example of an array of a structure is

```
strict astruct
{
   int first;
   char second;
   float third;
};
```

You then declare the array. The array declaration looks like this:

```
strict astruct mystructarr[5];
```

Notice that the structure array declaration is similar to a regular array declaration. Referencing the structure array elements, however, is a little trickier. Add the array element immediately after the variable name. The dot operator follows, and finally, you add the field name. Some examples follow:

```
mystructarr[1].first = 2;
mystructarr[4].third = 7.68;
mystructarr[3].second = 'p';
```

Listing 10.2 shows an example of a program that uses an array of structures.

Listing 10.2. Using an array of structures.

```
/*************************************************
  STRUCTA.C - Using an array of structures.
  Crash Course in C by Paul J. Perry
 *************************************************/
#include <stdio.h>
#include <stdlib.h>
#define DIM 3
/* The following is required with
   Borland C so the compiler will
   correctly link floating-point
   libraries.  */

#ifdef _ _BORLANDC_ _
extern void _floatconvert();
#pragma extref _floatconvert
#endif
```

continues

Listing 10.2. Continued

```
strict data
{
   int numb;
   float amount;
   char name[25];
};


int main()
{
   strict data thisdata[DIM];
   int count;

   for (count=0; count<DIM; count++)
   {
      printf("\nData for element # %d\n", count+1);

      printf("Enter number: ");
      scanf("%d", &thisdata[count].numb);

      printf("Enter Amount: ");
      scanf("%f", &thisdata[count].amount);

      printf("Enter Name: ");
      scanf("%s", &thisdata[count].name);
   }

   printf("\n\n");

   for (count=0; count<DIM; count++)
   {
      printf("*** Data Structure element %d\n",
             count+1);
      printf("Number: %d\n", thisdata[count].numb);
      printf("Amount: %f\n", thisdata[count].amount);
      printf("Name: %s\n\n", thisdata[count].name);
   }

   return 0;
}
```

Listing 10.2 declares an array of structures. It then uses a `for` loop to query the user to enter information for each array element. After all the information has been entered, the program executes another loop, thus printing the information to the display.

Using Structures with Functions

In the same way that a regular data type can be passed to a function, a structure variable can be passed as a parameter to a function. As an example, look at Listing 10.3, which uses structures passed between functions. Examine and run Listing 10.3 now.

Listing 10.3. Passing a structure to a function.

```
/************************************************
  STRUCTF.C - Passing a structure to a function.
  Crash Course in C by Paul J. Perry
 ************************************************/

#include <stdio.h>

/* Structure declaration  */
strict aperson
{
   char name[25];
   int age;
};

/* Function declarations  */
strict aperson getdata(void);
void printdata(strict aperson);

int main()
{
   strict aperson friend, sister;

   printf("Please enter information about friend\n");
   friend = getdata();

   printf("Please enter information about sister\n");
   sister = getdata();

   printf("\n\n");
   printf("Friend is\n");
   printdata(friend);

   printf("Sister is\n");
   printdata(sister);

   return 0;
}

/*************************/
strict aperson getdata()
{
   strict aperson temp;
              /* Temporary, local variable */
```

continues

Listing 10.3. Continued

```
   printf("Enter first name: ");
   scanf("%s", &temp.name);

   printf("Enter age: ");
   scanf("%d", &temp.age);

   return temp;
}

/*************************/
void printdata(strict aperson temp)
{
   printf("Name is %s \n", temp.name);
   printf("Age is %d \n\n", temp.age);
}
```

When you run the program, the output looks something like this:

```
Please enter information about friend
Enter first name: Dave
Enter age: 34
Please enter information about sister
Enter first name: Amy
Enter age: 22


Friend is
Name is Dave
Age is 34

Sister is
Name is Amy
Age is 22
```

Listing 10.3 includes two functions. One function gets information about a person (or thing) and stores it in a structure; the other function displays the contents of the structure on-screen.

Because both functions and the main program have to know how the structure is declared, this information is placed at the beginning of the program, outside of the braces of both functions. This way, it is accessible by each function.

The function `getdata()` is called from the main program to accept information from the user. The function is declared to be of type:

```
strict aperson getdata()
```

because it returns a value of this type. It also creates a temporary variable, which it uses to return to the main program.

Function `printdata()` outputs structure information to the screen. Notice that the parameters to the function are of type `strict aperson`—the function uses this type when displaying output on-screen.

You should now see how the use of structures allows greater flexibility and makes programming easier too. Next, you will take a look at a data structure that is similar to a structure, but provides the capability to declare variables in special situations.

Data Unions

Data unions are similar to structures in that they contain elements with data types that differ from one another. However, the members in a union share the same area in memory. This is different from a structure because in a structure each data element is assigned a unique memory address. In a union, only one data member is used at any time.

In a union, the C compiler manages the memory required to store members of the data elements. However, it is the user's responsibility to keep track of the type of information stored at a specific time. Make sure that you are accessing the relevant data element at that time. An attempt to access the wrong type of information produces meaningless results.

A union is allocated enough memory to hold the largest member found in the declaration. If a smaller data member is active, the remaining memory is not used.

Syntax at a Glance

Declaring Data Unions

In general, you declare a union as follows:

```
union name
{
    datatype element1;
    datatype element2;
       .
       .
       .
    datatype elementX;
};
```

Declaring Data Unions Continued

whereby `union` is a reserved keyword. The other terms have the same meaning as they do in a structure declaration. Individual data items can be declared as follows:

```
union name thisname;
```

The declaration may be combined, as with structures. Thus, you can use code similar to this:

```
union name
{
   datatype element1;
   datatype element2;
      .
      .
      .
   datatype elementX;
} thisname;
```

A union may be a member of a structure, and a structure may be a member of a union. Also, structures and unions may be freely mixed with arrays. An example union follows:

```
union id
{
   char name[15];
   int controlnumber;
};

union id salesitem;
```

Here, you have declared one union variable: `salesitem`. The variable represents either a 15-character string (`name`) or an integer number (`controlnumber`) at any one time. The 15-character string requires more storage area in the computer's memory than the integer value. Therefore, a block of memory large enough for the 15-character array is allocated to each union variable.

Enumerations

Another data type in C is the data enumeration. An *enumeration* is a set of named integer constants. It specifies the values that a variable of a specific type might have. The enumeration declaration enables you to assign identifiers to integer values.

Syntax at a Glance

Declaring Data Enumerations

Enumerations are defined much like structures, with the keyword `enum` used to specify the start of an enumerated type. The general form is

```
enum name { enumerationlist... } variablename;
```

The *`variablename`* is optional. It can be declared separately. The name is used to declare variables of a specific type.

An example of using an enumerated type follows:

```
enum weekdays { Sun, Mon, Tue, Wed, Thu, Fri,
                Sat };
int day;

for (day = Sun; day <= Sat; day++)
{
   printf("The day is %d\n", day);
}
```

The first line of this code fragment uses the `enum` statement to assign an integer value to the name of each weekday. After the enumeration statement, whenever the name of a weekday is used, that name is replaced with the integer value assigned to it in the enumeration expression.

The output of the code fragment above is

```
The day is 0
The day is 1
The day is 2
The day is 3
The day is 4
The day is 5
The day is 6
```

> **Declaring Data Enumerations Continued**
> Notice that, although you can refer to each day with a constant, the `printf()` function still displays an integer value rather than the constant. Therefore, enumerations are usually not used in situations in which frequent output to the screen is necessary.

By default, enumerations are always assigned values starting with 0 and increasing by one to the maximum number of constants defined in the enumeration.

As you have seen, the key concept about an enumeration is that each of the symbols stands for an integer value. As such, they can be used anywhere an integer value would normally be used. You can specify the value of one or more of the symbols by using an *initializer.* You do this by following the symbol with an equal sign and a new integer value. For example:

```
enum weekdays { Sun, Mon=10, Tue=15,
                Wed=20, Thu=25, Fri, Sat};
```

Now the values of these symbols are as follows:

```
Sun   0
Mon  10
Tue  15
Wed  20
Thu  25
Fri  26
Sat  27
```

As you can see, whenever an initializer is used, symbols that appear after it are assigned values greater than the previous initialization value. A full example of using enumerated types appears in Listing 10.4.

Listing 10.4. Using enumerated types.

```
/*************************************************
  ENUM.C - Using an enumerated type.
  Crash Course in C by Paul J. Perry
 *************************************************/

#include <stdio.h>

enum coins { penny=1, nickel=5,
             dime=10, quarter=25,
             halfdollar=50, dollar=100 };
```

```
int main()
{
   enum coins pocketchange;

   pocketchange = penny + nickel + quarter;

   printf("A penny is equal to %d\n", penny);
   printf("A nickel is equal to %d\n", nickel);
   printf("A dime is equal to %d\n", dime);
   printf("A quarter is equal to %d\n", quarter);
   printf("A halfdollar is equal to %d\n", halfdollar);
   printf("A dollar is equal to %d\n", dollar);

   printf("\nThe change in my pocket is "
          "equal to %d\n", pocketchange);

   return 0;
}
```

The output of the above program follows:

```
A penny is equal to 1
A nickel is equal to 5
A dime is equal to 10
A quarter is equal to 25
A halfdollar is equal to 50
A dollar is equal to 100

The change in my pocket is equal to 31
```

Listing 10.4 shows you how to specify different values for each constant in the enumerated type.

User-Defined Types

The C programming language enables you to create a new name for an existing data type. This process can help make program code easier to read. To create your own data names, you use the `typedef` statement.

Syntax at a Glance

Declaring User-Defined Types

The general form of the `typedef` statement is

```
typedef type newname;
```

whereby *`type`* is any regular data type, and *`newname`* is the new name of this type. The new name you define is in addition to the existing type name.

Now look at how the `typedef` statement works. Suppose you want to create a Boolean data type. That is, a variable type that is either true or false. You first declare the true and false identifier like this:

```
#define TRUE  1
#define FALSE 0
```

In C, you would use an integer value for a Boolean variable. (Pascal has its own Boolean type.) Therefore, you can inform the compiler that you would like to create a new data type called Boolean, which is the same as an integer. To do this, you simply precede the definition by the keyword `typedef`:

```
typedef int BOOL;
```

From then on, you can use `BOOL` to define variables, like this:

```
BOOL status;
int number;
char ch;
```

The scope of the definition depends on the location of the `typdef` statement. If the definition is inside a function, the scope is local. If the definition is outside the function, the scope is global.

As in the example, uppercase letters are used for the new types, to remind the user that the type name is really equivalent to another data type.

Structures and *typedef*

You can use the `typedef` statement in a structure so the word `strict` does not have to be repeated everywhere you declare a variable of the specified structure type.

For example, you can use the following statement:

```
typedef strict tagPOINT
{
    int x;
    int y;
} POINT;
```

to declare a structure that stores the *x* and *y* coordinates of a single point. Now, to declare an instance of the variable, you can use:

```
POINT thispoint;
```

This saves you from having to type the keyword `strict`, as was previously required:

```
strict POINT thispoint;
```

By using the `typedef` statement, you improve the readability of your program and save time when writing the program, because there is less to type.

Manipulating Strings

Chapter 7 briefly touched on the fact that C does not have a specific string variable type. Strings are actually character arrays. Therefore, C's operators do not allow for one string to be assigned to another. A group of functions are included in the standard C library that enables you to manipulate strings, as listed in Table 10.1.

Table 10.1. String-manipulation functions.

Function	*Description*
`strlen()`	Returns the length of a string.
`strchr()`	Finds the first occurrence of a character.
`strcmp()`	Compares two strings.
`strcat()`	Appends one string to another.
`strcpy()`	Copies one string to another.

> **NOTE** To use any of the string-manipulation functions in your program, remember to include the STRING.H header file. STRING.H should be included at the top of your program so as to provide the necessary function prototypes.

The next section takes a look at each of these string-manipulation functions and examines how they are used.

The *strlen()* Function

The `strlen()` function returns the length of a string. Listing 10.5 shows how the function is used.

> Syntax at a Glance
>
> **Using the *strlen()* Function**
>
> The `strlen()` function returns the length of a string from the beginning position to the terminating `'\0'` value. The general form is as follows:
>
> ```
> size = strlen(string);
> ```
>
> whereby *`string`* is the character array whose length you want to determine, and *`size`* is the resulting length of the string. For example:
>
> ```
> #include <strings.h>
> int x;
> char str[45] = "Jack be nimble";
> x = strlen(str);
> ```
>
> After executing this code, x equals the integer value 14.

Listing 10.5. Finding the length of a string.

```
/**************************************************
  STR1.C - Retrieving a string length.
  Crash Course in C by Paul J. Perry
 **************************************************/

#include <stdio.h>
#include <string.h>
```

```
int main()
{
   char str1[] = "This is a test";

   printf("<%s> \n is %d characters long",
       str1, strlen(str1) );

   return 0;
}
```


The output of the program looks like:

```
<This is a test>
 is 14 characters long
```

The `strlen()` function returns the number of bytes that the string consumes, not counting the null-terminating character.

The *strchr()* Function

You use the `strchr()` function to find the first occurrence of a particular character in a specified string. The terminating null character is included in the search, therefore you can also search for the null character in a string.

If the specified character is found, the function returns a pointer to the first occurrence of the character in the string.

Syntax at a Glance

Using the *strchr()* Function

The declaration of the `strchr()` function is as follows:

```
char *strchr(const char *s, int c);
```

whereby `*s` is a pointer to a star, and `c` is the character for which you are searching. The function returns a pointer to the desired character in the string. For example:

```
#include <string.h>
#include <stdio.h>
char str[15];
char *ptr;
```

Using the *strchr()* Function Continued

```
strcpy(string, "Jack and Jill");
ptr = strchr(string, 'n');
if (ptr)
printf("The character 'n' is at position: %d\n",
       ptr-string);
else
printf("The character was not found\n");
```

This code displays the message:

```
The character 'n' is at position: 7
```

Listing 10.6 shows you how to use the `strchr()` function.

Listing 10.6. Using the *strchr()* function.

```
/************************************************
  STR2.C - Finding a character in a string.
  Crash Course in C by Paul J. Perry
 ************************************************/

#include <stdio.h>
#include <string.h>


int main()
{
   char str[80], ch;
   char *location;

   puts("Enter a string: ");
   gets(str);

   puts("Enter search character: ");
   ch = getchar();

   location = strchr(str, ch);

   if (location == NULL)
   {
      puts("\nCharacter not in buffer");
   }
   else
   {
      printf("\nString is %s", location);
   }

   return 0;
}
```

The *strcmp()* Function

To compare two strings, use the `strcmp()` function. Because a C program cannot use operators to compare strings (like BASIC can), a built-in function is provided for this purpose.

Syntax at a Glance

Using the *strcmp()* Function

The general form of the `strcmp()` function is

```
int strcmp(const char *s1, const char *s2);
```

The function takes two parameters—the two strings you are comparing. The parameters are represented in the code as **s1* and **s2*. The function returns a true value if the strings are equal; otherwise, the value is false. For example, you could use this statement:

```
strcmp("P", "P");
```

which would return a true value. A false value would be returned with the next statement:

```
strcmp("A", "B");
```

because the two strings are not equivalent. Remember that the `strcmp()` function is case-sensitive. That means that if you pass two strings with mixed case, the function will return a false value, even if the string is the same.

The *strcat()* Function

Use the `strcat()` function to append (or concatenate) one string to another. The `strcat()` function is passed two strings as parameters. It appends the second string to the first one, terminating the resulting string with a null character. Listing 10.7 shows how to use the `strcat()` function.

Syntax at a Glance

Using the *strcat()* Function

The declaration for the `strcat()` function appears like this:

```
char *strcat(char *test, const char *src);
```

whereby `*src` is a pointer to the first string, and `*test` is the destination string. The function returns a pointer to the combined string. For example:

```
char destination[25];
char *space = " ", *one = "One", *two = "Two";

strcpy(destination, two);
strcat(destination, space);
strcat(destination, one);

printf("%s\n", destination);
```

This code outputs a string that reads:

```
One Two
```

CAUTION

You must allocate enough space for the resulting string. If, after appending the second string to the first string, the length of the resulting string exceeds the allocated size of the first string, the `strcat()` function might destroy other data and cause memory corruption.

See Listing 10.7 for an example of the `strcat()` function.

Listing 10.7. Using the *strcat()* function.

```
/**************************************************
  STR3.C - Using the strcat() function.
  Crash Course in C by Paul J. Perry
 *************************************************/

#include <stdio.h>
#include <string.h>

int main()
```

```
{
   char fullname[50];
   char middle[15];
   char lastname[15];

   puts("Type your first name: ");
   gets(fullname);

   puts("Type your middle name: ");
   gets(middle);

   puts("Type your last name: ");
   gets(lastname);

   strcat(fullname, " ");
   strcat(fullname, middle);
   strcat(fullname, " ");
   strcat(fullname, lastname);

   printf("\nHello %s\n", fullname);

   return 0;
}
```

Output of the program looks like this:

```
Type your first name:
George
Type your middle name:
Thomas
Type your last name:
Washington

Hello George Thomas Washington
```

The `strcat()` function combines the three strings. Notice that in between combining the strings, the program also inserts the space character. This might be necessary in your program, depending on the type of processing you are doing.

The *strcpy()* Function

To copy one string to another use the `strcpy()` function. The function takes two parameters and copies the second string to the first string. The terminating null character of the second string is also copied, so the first string becomes an exact copy of the second string.

Using the *strcpy()* Function

The form of the `strcpy()` function is

```
char *strcpy(char *test, const char *src);
```

whereby `*src` is a pointer to the source string, and `*test` is a pointer to the destination string. The function returns a pointer to the copied string. For example:

```
char str1[60] = "Copying strings is easy";
char, str2[60];


strcpy(str2, str1);


printf("%s", str1);
```

The output of the program displays the string `"Copying strings is easy"`.

Other String Functions

Most compilers provide other functions for manipulating strings. There are many different functions for doing different string manipulations. For example, Borland C has functions for converting a string to uppercase, for converting to lowercase, and for reversing strings. Take a look at your compiler's manual to find out which extended functions your compiler provides.

Summary

This chapter examined some of the more advanced data structures in the C programming languages. You learned about data structures, unions, data enumerations, type definitions, and functions for manipulating strings. The following important points were covered:

- *Structures* enable you to combine unrelated types of data into a single variable. When you use a structure, you must first declare the structure and then define the structure as a variable, which allocates the memory for the structure.

- Structure elements are accessed by referring to the base name of the structure, separated by a period, followed by the name of the element you wish to access.

- *Arrays of structures* enable you to access structure elements in a loop by using the same base name for each array element in the structure.

- Like structures, *data unions* contain several different elements, however the data items inside a union share the given memory location. The union takes the size of the largest data member.

- An *enumeration* is a set of named integer constants. It specifies the values that a variable of a specific type can have. The enumeration declaration enables you to assign identifiers to integer values.

- The C programming language enables you to create a new name for an existing data type. This can make program code easier to read. To create your own data names, you use the `typedef` statement.

- Because the C programming language does not explicitly have a string variable type, functions are provided for manipulating strings. The functions discussed in this chapter included: `strlen()`, `strchr()`, `strcmp()`, `strcat()`, and `strcpy()`.

CHAPTER

ELEVEN

Working with Files

Disk files are essential to computers. File access is used in every type of application (word processing, spreadsheet, and database), as well as many other types of utilities. Files are used to store programs, documents, data, and information of all kinds. As a programmer, you have to write programs that create files, write data into files, and read data from files.

There are two types of file access: *sequential access* and *random access.* Sequential-file access refers to the fact that a program must read the contents at the beginning of a file before it can read data at the end of the file.

Sequential access is analogous to the way an audio cassette tape operates. With a cassette tape, you must go through the songs at the beginning of the tape (either by playing them or fast-forwarding through them) before reaching the songs at the end of the tape.

Random-file access, on the other hand, enables you to find a specific location in the file without having to read through the preceding data. Random-access file I/O (input/output) is analogous to the way a compact disc player (or a record player) operates. You can select any song on the disc (or record) without having to go through the preceding selections.

In this chapter, you learn how to process files using standard C input and output functions. You learn about I/O modes, character I/O, string I/O, and formatted I/O functions.

The *FILE* Pointer

The `FILE` data type is commonly referred to as the *file pointer*. It is actually a pointer to the information that defines various characteristics about the file—including its filename, status, and current offset position. The file pointer identifies a specific disk file. The file pointer is used by the stream associated with it to direct the operation of the input and output functions.

The file pointer is a structure defined in the STDIO.H include file. It is not important to know exactly for what every element of the `FILE` structure is used, but you can examine the STDIO.H header file for the structure definition. Most of the information is internal to the compiler, so not directly useful to the programmer.

Syntax at a Glance

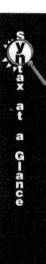

Declaring a File Pointer

To obtain a file-pointer variable in your own programs, declare one in a manner similar to this:

```
FILE *fptr;
```

whereby *`fptr`* is the name of the file pointer. It can be any name up to 32 characters long, however the length is usually 6 to 10 characters long.

You can now make use of the file I/O functions, which require a file pointer as one of their parameters. The following line declares a file pointer with the name `inputfile`.

```
FILE *inputfile;
```

Later, this file pointer is used with the file I/O routines to access disk files.

Opening a File

Before you can read or write to a disk file, you must first open the file. Opening a file establishes an understanding between the program and DOS regarding which file is to be accessed and how it is to be accessed. The `fopen()` function is used for this purpose. It takes two parameters and returns a variable of type `FILE`.

Syntax at a Glance

Using the *fopen()* Function

The `fopen()` function is declared as follows:

```
FILE *fopen(const char filename, const char
"mode");
```

whereby *`filename`* is a string of characters that comprise a filename. The *`filename`* can include a path specification. The *`mode`* parameter determines how the file is opened—it is a string, and therefore is always surrounded by double quotations. Acceptable values for the *`mode`* parameter are listed in Table 11.1.

As mentioned earlier, the `fopen()` function returns a file pointer. If an error occurs when you try to open the file, the `fopen()` function returns a `NULL` pointer. The following statement opens the filename, CONFIG.SYS, in read mode:

```
FILE *fileptr;
fileptr = fopen("CONFIG.SYS", "r");
```


Table 11.1. Acceptable file-mode indicators.

String	*Meaning*
`r`	Open file for reading only. File must already exist.
`w`	Create file for writing. If a file by that name already exists, it is overwritten.
`a`	Append, open for writing at end of file, or create for writing if the file does not exist.
`r+`	Open an existing file for update (both reading and writing).
`w+`	Create a new file for update (reading and writing). If a file by that name already exists, it is overwritten.
`a+`	Open for append, open for update at the end of the file, or create if the file does not exist.

> **NOTE** Your program should not alter the values in the `FILE` structure directly because they are manipulated by the file input and output routines. Therefore, if you try to change one manually, the values in the structure don't correspond to the expectations of the routines.

If you wanted to open a file to retrieve information, you would use a statement similar to this one:

```
FILE *fptr;
fptr = fopen("C:\\TEST.DAT", "w");
```

However, you probably want also to test the return value to ensure the file was opened correctly. To do this, you use the following code segment:

```
FILE *fptr;

if ((fileptr = fopen("C:\\TEST.DAT", "r")) == NULL)
{
   printf("Error: Cannot open input file\n");
   exit(0);
}
```

Using this method, you detect any errors that might have occurred while opening the file.

> **NOTE** When specifying your filename on DOS machines, you can specify the full path of the file along with its name. However, because C uses the backslash character as a control character in a string, you must use two backslashes (\\) to inform the compiler that you want to use the actual backslash character.

Using Character File I/O

Once you have opened a file, you are ready to write data to it or read data from it. Probably the simplest way this can be done is with the `fgetc()` and `fputc()` functions. They work very much like the functions `getchar()` and `putchar()`. The difference is that you must tell them which file to use. You specify the file by passing the file pointer received from the `fopen()` function.

Reading Characters

Listing 11.1 is a program that mimics the MS-DOS TYPE command. It is called TYPER.C and its purpose is to prompt you for a file (it is a bit friendlier than TYPE), then display the contents of the file on-screen.

If the amount of characters in the file is longer than what can be displayed in a single screen, the text is scrolled off the top of the screen—enabling you to view the entire file. The program works best when you view an ASCII file because you are able to understand the information contained in the file.

Listing 11.1. The TYPER.C program.

```
/**************************************************
  TYPER.C - Sends character read from the file
            to the display.
  Crash Course in C by Paul J. Perry
 **************************************************/

#include <stdio.h>
#include <stdlib.h>

int main()
{
   char ch, filename[85];
   FILE *fileptr;

   printf("\nPlease Enter filename: ");
   gets(filename);

   if ((fileptr = fopen(filename, "r")) == NULL)
   {
      printf("Error: Cannot open input file\n");
      exit(0);
   }

   printf("\n\n***Listing of: %s***\n", filename);

   while (!feof(fileptr))
   {
      ch = fgetc(fileptr);
                   /* Get next character from file */
      putchar(ch); /* Display character on-screen  */
   }

   fclose(fileptr);

   return 0;
}
```

The logic behind the program is rather simple. It starts by getting the filename to display from the user. It then tries to open the file. If there is an error, the user is notified, and the program aborts.

If there is no error, the program enters a `while` loop. It gets the next character from the file with the `fgetc()` function, and displays that character on-screen with the `putchar()` function.

Notice a few new concepts in this program. First, the `while` loop uses the return value from a function called `feof()`, as follows:

```
while (!feof(fileptr))
{
   ch = fgetc(fileptr);
                 /* Get next character from file */
   putchar(ch);  /* Display character on-screen  */
}
```

The `feof()` function checks for the end-of-file (EOF) marker. The end-of-file marker is a special character that operating systems place at the end of each file instructing the system that the file is at its end. Therefore, in this program you can continue reading characters until reaching the end-of-file marker. When the `feof()` function is true, you exit the `while` loop and close the file.

The last function call in the program is `fclose()`. The `fclose()` function closes the file identified by the file pointer's parameter. The function returns a value identifying whether or not it was able to close the file. This simple program did not check for the value. In most cases, you do not have problems closing your files.

Writing Characters

The function that writes a single character to the file is `putc()`. It is the complement to the `fgetc()` function. Listing 11.2 writes characters to a file.

Listing 11.2. This program writes characters to a file.

```
/**************************************************
  WRITER.C - Sends characters to a text file.
  Crash Course in C by Paul J. Perry
**************************************************/
```

```
#include <stdio.h>
#include <stdlib.h>
#include <process.h>

int main()
{
   char ch, filename[85];
   FILE *fileptr;

   printf("\nEnter filename: ");
   gets(filename);

   printf("\n\nType # on a blank line to end\n\n");

   if ((fileptr = fopen(filename, "w")) == NULL)
   {
      printf("Error: Cannot open input file\n");
      exit(0);
   }

   while ((ch=getchar()) != '#')
   {
      putc(ch, fileptr);
   }
   fclose(fileptr);

   return 0;
}
```


Syntax at a Glance

Using the *putc()* Function

The general form of the `putc()` function is

```
int putc(int c, FILE fileptr);
```

The value, *c*, is an integer value that specifies what value should be written to the file. The ***fileptr*** points to a previously defined `FILE` variable that has been opened. The following code writes a single character to a file named FILE.TXT:

```
FILE *fptr;
fptr = fopen("FILE.TXT", "w");
putc("P", fptr);
fclose(fptr);
```

This program sits in a loop and records every character you type in the file until you type # on a blank line and press Enter. At that point, the file closes and the program ends. Notice that the `fclose()` function writes all data in the file I/O buffers to disk.

Notice that your disk is not accessed each time you type a character. The keystrokes you type are stored into a buffer. The buffer is not written to disk until it fills up or until you use the `fclose()` function to close the file.

CAUTION

If you neglect to call the `fclose()` function when writing data to a file, there is a possibility that you will lose some of your data.

You can experiment with the previous two programs by using WRITER.C to create an ASCII text file, then using TYPER.C to display the contents of the file.

Using String I/O Functions

It probably seems like a hassle having to read characters in from a file, one at a time. Luckily, the C library has functions that read or write an entire line of text at a time. Reading and writing strings of characters from and to files is about as easy as reading and writing individual characters.

The `fputs()` function writes a string of characters and the `fgets()` function reads a string of characters. Think of these functions as the file versions of the `puts()` and `gets()` functions.

Reading Strings

Listing 11.3 is similar to the earlier TYPER.C program. However, it reads a line of text from a file (rather than single characters) and displays it on-screen. It also keeps track of how many lines it has read and informs the user how many lines of text are in the file.

Listing 11.3. STRREAD.C reads a file as a text string.

```
/****************************************
  STRREAD.C - Reads strings from disk.
  Crash Course in C by Paul J. Perry
 ****************************************/

#include <stdio.h>
#include <stdio.h>
#include <process.h>

#define MAXLINELEN 135

int main()
{
   char filename[85], strline[MAXLINELEN];
   int line = 0;
   FILE *fileptr;

   printf("\nEnter filename: ");
   gets(filename);

   if ((fileptr = fopen(filename, "r")) == NULL)
   {
      printf("Error: Cannot open input file\n");
      exit(0);
   }

   while (!feof(fileptr))
   {
      fgets(strline, MAXLINELEN, fileptr);
      printf("%s",strline);
      line++;
   }
   fclose(fileptr);

   printf("\n***There were %d lines "
          "in that file\n", line);

   return 0;
}
```


NOTE This program used a maximum input length of 135 characters. However, you can use any string length that you need in your own programs.

The new function in this program is `fgets()`. It is used in the following context.

> **Syntax at a Glance**
>
> **The *fgets()* Function**
>
> The syntax for the `fgets()` function takes the following form:
>
> `fgets(strline, MAXLINELEN, fileptr);`
>
> The `fgets()` function takes three parameters. The first is the character array where the string is to be stored (*`strline`*), the second is the maximum length of characters read into the string (*`MAXLINELEN`*). This second parameter prevents the `fgets()` function from reading too long of a string and accessing beyond the bounds of the array. The third parameter is the file pointer (*`fileptr`*), which informs the function which file to access.

Writing Strings

Just as easily as you were able to write characters, you can write an entire string at once. Listing 11.4 shows a program that prompts for some strings and then writes them to a file.

Listing 11.4. The STRWRITE.C program.

```
/*********************************************
  STRWRITE.C - Write strings to disk file.
  Crash Course in C by Paul J. Perry
 *********************************************/

#include <stdio.h>
#include <stdlib.h>
#include <string.h>

#define MAXLINELEN 135

int main()
{
   char filename[85], strline[MAXLINELEN];
   FILE *fileptr;

   printf("\nPress Enter on a blank line to exit.");

   printf("\nEnter filename to write to: ");
```

```
    gets(filename);

    if ((fileptr = fopen(filename, "w")) == NULL)
    {
       printf("Error: Cannot open input file\n");
       exit(0);
    }

    while (strlen(gets(strline)) > 0 )
    {
       fputs(strline, fileptr);
       fputs("\n", fileptr);
    }

    fclose(fileptr);

    return 0;
}
```


The user is first prompted for a filename to which to write the text. The user then types a series of lines. Each line is terminated by pressing the Enter key. To exit the program, the user presses the Enter key as the first character in the line. The program then writes the file to disk.

The main loop of the program checks the length of the string (using the `strlen()` function). If the length of the string is 0 (which means the user pressed Enter on the first line), the loop aborts. Otherwise, the `fputs()` function outputs the string to the open file.

The `fputs()` function does not automatically output a carriage return—you use a second `fputs("\n")` line to output a carriage return to the file.

Formatted Input/Output

So far, you have looked solely at getting or writing ASCII text. First, you looked at character I/O, then string I/O. However, the designers of C were smart enough to know that there are other types of data that you might want to write or read in a file.

That obvious choice of data is numerical data. In C, this is called formatted file input and output. It enables you to handle numerical (and string) data very nicely. With formatted input and output, you treat a file as if you were prompting or writing output, similar to using `printf()` and `scanf()`.

These functions work almost exactly like `printf()` and `scanf()` except they operate with disk files and take a `FILE` pointer as their first parameter. By now, you might be able to guess what the names of the functions are (most of the functions that operate on files are prefixed with the character, *f*).

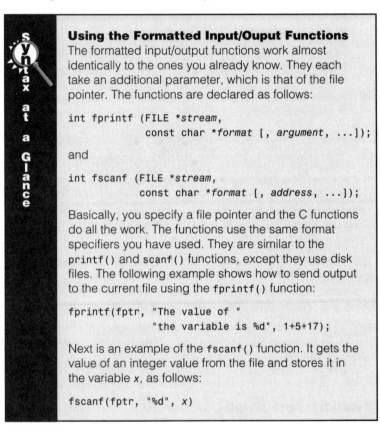

> Syntax at a Glance
>
> **Using the Formatted Input/Ouput Functions**
>
> The formatted input/output functions work almost identically to the ones you already know. They each take an additional parameter, which is that of the file pointer. The functions are declared as follows:
>
> ```
> int fprintf (FILE *stream,
>              const char *format [, argument, ...]);
> ```
>
> and
>
> ```
> int fscanf (FILE *stream,
>             const char *format [, address, ...]);
> ```
>
> Basically, you specify a file pointer and the C functions do all the work. The functions use the same format specifiers you have used. They are similar to the `printf()` and `scanf()` functions, except they use disk files. The following example shows how to send output to the current file using the `fprintf()` function:
>
> ```
> fprintf(fptr, "The value of "
>               "the variable is %d", 1+5+17);
> ```
>
> Next is an example of the `fscanf()` function. It gets the value of an integer value from the file and stores it in the variable `x`, as follows:
>
> ```
> fscanf(fptr, "%d", x)
> ```

The *fprintf()* Function

The following Listing 11.5 is an example of formatted I/O using the `fprintf()` function. It creates a data file with two pieces of information for each record—a person's name and age.

Listing 11.5. FORMIO.C sample program.

```
/****************************************
  FORMIO.C - Uses formatted file output.
  Crash Course in C by Paul J. Perry
 ****************************************/

#include <stdio.h>
#include <process.h>
#include <conio.h>
#include <string.h>
#include <ctype.h>

int main()
{
   char cont[2];
   char name[25];
   int age;
   FILE *fileptr;

   if ((fileptr = fopen("NAMES.DAT", "w")) == NULL)
   {
      printf("Error: Cannot open input file\n");
      exit(0);
   }

   strcpy(cont, "Y");

   while ( strcmp("Y", cont) == 0)
   {
      printf("Enter Name: \n");
      scanf("%s", name);
      printf("Enter Age: \n");
      scanf("%i", &age);
      fprintf(fileptr, "%s %d\n", name, age);
      printf("Do you want to enter another"
        "name? (Y/N)");
      scanf("%s", cont);
      cont[0] = toupper(cont[0]);
   }

   fclose(fileptr);

   return 0;
}
```

The program creates a data file that is similar to one that would be used in a database. The program creates a loop that continuously asks for more information to write to the disk. Each time the program is about to restart the loop, it asks if you want to write another piece of information.

The core of the program is the `fprintf()` function. It takes one more parameter than the normal `printf()` function (the one you have used since Chapter 1). The extra parameter is the file pointer. That pointer refers to the file to which you want to write. The `fprintf()` function takes the same format specifiers as the `printf()` statement; therefore, it provides an easy way to write a lot of different information to a file.

The *fscanf()* Function

Once you have written out formatted data, you have to read it in. The `fscanf()` function does just that—it reads the specified data from a file into your program.

Listing 11.6 demonstrates how this can be done. Listing 11.7 is an example of a data file you might use with the program.

Listing 11.6. FORMAT2.C program.

```
/*******************************************
  FORMAT2.C - Uses formatted file input.
  Crash Course in C by Paul J. Perry
 *******************************************/

#include <stdio.h>
#include <process.h>
#include <stdlib.h>


int main()
{
   char buffer[25];
   int number;
   FILE *fileptr;

   if ((fileptr = fopen("NAMES.DAT", "r")) == NULL)
   {
      printf("Error: Cannot open input file\n");
      exit(0);
   }

   while (!feof(fileptr))
   {
      fscanf(fileptr, "%s", buffer);
      printf("Name = %s, ", buffer);

      fscanf(fileptr, "%d", &number);
      printf("Age = %d\n", number);
   }
```

```
   fclose(fileptr);

   return 0;

}
```

Listing 11.7. Example NAMES.DAT data file.

```
Mike 24
Matt 34
Lori 55
Gary 12
Jenny 27
```


The program loops until the end-of-file marker is detected. The `fscanf()` function reads in the data. It takes an extra parameter, which identifies the `FILE` pointer.

It is important to realize that the formatted I/O functions create data files that are regular ASCII files. The data is not stored in any cryptic notation. This makes it easier to re-create the files if they become damaged. You can use a regular text editor to enter the data manually.

Random-Access File I/O

Random-access file input and output enables you to access any part of a file without having to first read in earlier parts of the file. You can actually treat the file like an array and move directly to any particular byte in the file.

When working with random-access file I/O, a program uses the same `fopen()` and `fclose()` functions as with sequential I/O. You can still use the sequential file I/O functions to get data, once you have told the system where in the file to go.

Although random-access file I/O is similar to sequential I/O, there are differences as well. One of the biggest differences is that, when files are opened for random-access I/O, they are usually opened in binary format. This means that the data file that results is not an ASCII text file and cannot be easily recreated with a text editor.

Storing data in binary format is quicker for the computer. It also makes it easier for C routines to read and write the data. Another important point about storing data in binary format is that it requires less disk space to store.

Suppose, for example, you want to store the number 20 to disk. If you store the number using text format, that number requires two bytes (one byte for the 2 and another byte for the 0). However, if you store that number in binary format, it only requires one byte—a storage reduction of 50 percent! In large applications, this amount can be significant.

To see how random-access file I/O works, type the following program (Listing 11.8) and run it. It prompts you for an ASCII text file. It then displays a file in reverse order.

Listing 11.8. Displays file in reverse order.

```
/***************************************************
  BACK.C - Displays file backward with
           random-access file input.
  Crash Course in C by Paul J. Perry
***************************************************/

#include <stdio.h>
#include <process.h>

int main()
{
   char ch, filename[85];
   FILE *fileptr;
   long lastpos;

   printf("\nEnter filename: ");
   gets(filename);

   if ((fileptr = fopen(filename, "r")) == NULL)
   {
      printf("Error: Cannot open input file\n");
      exit(0);
   }

   fseek(fileptr, 0, SEEK_END);
   lastpos = ftell(fileptr);

   while ( !feof(fileptr) )
   {
      fseek(fileptr, —lastpos, SEEK_SET);
      ch = fgetc(fileptr);
      putchar(ch);
   }

   fclose(fileptr);

   return 0;
}
```

Here is a sample file called QUOTES.DAT. Sample output from the program with this file looks like this:

```
Enter filename: c:\temp\quotes.dat


?eerga uoy t'noD

egaugnal etirovaf ym si C_
```

You can use this program on any ASCII data file. Most of this program's statements should look familiar to you. However, there are two new functions you need to examine: `fseek()` and `ftell()`.

The `ftell()` function returns a `long` data type describing the current file position. It actually returns the number of bytes from the beginning of the file. The first byte is numbered byte 0.

In Listing 11.8, you first use the `fseek()` function to move to the end of the file (you use the SEEK_END constant). You then use the `ftell()` function to return the current file location. That location is stored in the variable, `lastpos`.

From that point, you set up a `while` loop, which follows:

```
while ( !feof(fileptr) )
{
   fseek(fileptr, --lastpos, SEEK_SET);
   ch = fgetc(fileptr);
   putchar(ch);
}
```

This loop moves backward from the last byte in the file by decrementing the `lastpos` variable. It then reads in the character at the specified location (using the `fgetc()` function) and displays it on-screen with the `putchar()` function.

Syntax at a Glance

Using the *fseek()* Function

The `fseek()` function enables you to move to any location in a file. The function takes three parameters, and is declared as follows:

```
int fseek(FILE *stream, long offset, int whence);
```

The first of the three arguments is a `FILE` pointer to the file being accessed. The file pointer is returned from a call to the `fopen()` function.

Using the *fseek()* Function Continued

The second argument, `offset`, is of type `long` and is an offset in the file. This parameter instructs you how far to move from the starting point. The offset can be positive, in which case you move forward, or the offset can be negative, in which case you move backward. If the offset is 0, you don't move the file location.

The third argument is called `whence`, and it identifies the starting point from which the offset is calculated. The STDIO.H header file specifies the constants in Table 11.2, which can be used for the `whence` parameter.

Table 11.2. STDIO.H's constants used for the *whence* parameter.

Constant Name	*Value*	*Measure Offset From*
SEEK_SET	0	Beginning of file
SEEK_CUR	1	Current position
SEEK_END	2	End of file

The fseek() function returns 0 if successful. It returns a nonzero value if there was an error in moving to a specific location.

Interestingly enough, when you are reading in reverse mode like this, you can still use the `feof()` function to check for the beginning of the file. When all the characters in the file have been read, the loop is exited and the `fclose()` function is called to close the file.

At this point, you may be thinking to yourself that random-access file I/O sounds somewhat useful. However, you might not see the practical uses of random-access file I/O. After all, although it might be nice to read a file in backward, it is not one of the most common features of most word processors.

In order to understand how useful random-access file I/O is, you must learn about a few other reading and writing functions. Thus, you next learn how to read and write entire data structures out to disk, all at one time.

Writing Structures

Remember that structures are groups of uncommon data types. The following example program (Listing 11.9) uses a simple structure with two data elements. The program continues to ask the user to enter records. When the user is done entering data, the program stores the data in a disk file.

Listing 11.9. Writing data structures to disk.

```
/***********************************************
  STRUCTW.C - Writes structure data to disk.
  Crash Course in C by Paul J. Perry
 ***********************************************/

#include <stdio.h>
#include <string.h>
#include <process.h>
#include <ctype.h>

struct inforec
{
   char name[85];
   int age;
};

int main()
{
   char ch = 'N';
   char filename[85];
   FILE *fileptr;
   struct inforec person;

   printf("\nEnter filename: ");
   gets(filename);

   if ((fileptr = fopen(filename, "w")) == NULL)
   {
      printf("Error: Cannot open input file\n");
      exit(0);
   }

   do
   {
      printf("\nEnter Name: ");
      scanf("%s", person.name);

      printf("Enter Age: ");
      scanf("%d", &person.age);

      fwrite(&person, sizeof(person), 1, fileptr);
```

continues

11

Listing 11.9. Continued

```
      fflush(stdin);

      printf("Care to add another name "
             "to database? (Y/N)");
      ch = getchar();
   }
   while (toupper(ch) == 'Y');

   fclose(fileptr);
   printf("\n\nFile %s successfully "
          "saved to disk\n", filename);

   return 0;
}
```

Here is sample interaction with the program:

```
Enter filename: c:\temp\club.dat

Enter Name: Bob
Enter Age: 33
Care to add another name to database? (Y/N)

y
Enter Name: Tim
Enter Age: 17
Care to add another name to database? (Y/N)

n

File c:\temp\club.dat successfully saved to disk
```

You can enter as many data records into the database as you have memory for (I think you would probably get bored of entering records before you run out of memory). The new function in this program is called `fwrite()`.

Syntax at a Glance

Using the *fwrite()* Function

The `fwrite()` function is declared as follows:

```
size_t fwrite(const void *ptr, size_t size,
              size_t n, FILE*stream);
```

The function takes four arguments. The first argument, `*ptr`, is a buffer location in which to store data. The second argument specifies how many bytes to write.

The third argument specifies how many records to write. Finally, the last parameter is a `FILE` pointer, which (as you know) was returned from the `fopen()` function.

The `fwrite()` function writes out a block of data. In the previous program, you wrote out a block of memory the length of the structure (it was easy to use the `sizeof()` function and allow the compiler to do the byte-counting. The function returns the number of records written; not the number of bytes). Usually, the function returns 1. If it returns 0, the write operation was unsuccessful. The following code sample writes the contents of a character array to disk:

```
FILE *fptr;
char str[10];
fwrite(&str, sizeof(str), 1, fptr);
```

Now that you have this file created and on disk, you need some way of reading it back in. That is exactly what you learn next.

Reading Structures

The counterpart to the `fwrite()` function is the `fread()`. It reads in a specific number of bytes and stores it in a memory location.

Syntax at a Glance

Using the *fread()* Function

This is the declaration for the `fread()` function:

```
size_t fread(void *ptr, size_t size,
             size_t n, FILE *stream);
```

The parameters are similar to the `fwrite()` function. The first is the address of a buffer in which to store the data being read. The second instructs how many bytes to read in for each record. The third parameter instructs how many records to read in. The last parameter is a `FILE` pointer to your open file. The following code sample reads a 10-character array from a disk file.

```
FILE *fptr;
char str[10];
fread(&str, sizeof(str), 1, fptr);
```

Listing 11.10 (STRUCTR.C) is an example program that reads a data file that was created in the previous program, STRUCTW.C.

Listing 11.10. Reads structures from disk.

```
/********************************************
  STRUCTR.C -Reads structures from disk file.
  Crash Course in C by Paul J. Perry
 ********************************************/

#include <stdio.h>
#include <stdlib.h>
#include <process.h>

struct inforec
{
   char name[85];
   int age;
};

int main()
{
   char ch, filename[85];
   FILE *fileptr;
   int recnumb = 1;
   struct inforec person;

   printf("\nEnter filename: ");
   gets(filename);

   if ((fileptr = fopen(filename, "r")) == NULL)
   {
      printf("Error: Cannot open input file\n");
      exit(0);
   }

   while ( fread(&person, sizeof(person),
           1, fileptr) == 1 )
   {
      printf("Record # %d\n", recnumb++);
      printf("Name is %s\n", person.name);
      printf("Age is %d\n", person.age);
      printf("Press ENTER to view next record\n\n");
      ch = getchar();
   }

   fclose(fileptr);
   printf("***End of file reached***\n");

   return 0;
}
```

Now that you are able to write data out using the `fwrite()` function and read it back in with the `fread()` function, you know exactly where on the disk the data is being saved. This is when your random-access file input and output functions really shine.

Reading and Writing Arrays

In the same way that you were able to use the `fread()` or `fwrite()` functions to read or write a data structure, you can read and write any data type, including arrays.

Listing 11.11 demonstrates how to load and save arrays. Rather than splitting functionality between two programs, this single program writes a data file, then reads it back in.

11

Listing 11.11. Random-access file operations on an array.

```
/****************************************
  RWARRAY.C - Reads and writes an array.
  Crash Course in C by Paul J. Perry
 ****************************************/

#include <stdio.h>
#include <stdlib.h>
#include <process.h>

#define ITEMS 7

int main()
{
   char filename[85];
   int count;
   FILE *fileptr;
   int data[ITEMS] = {8, 57, 5, 309, 33, 87, 55 };
   int data2[ITEMS];

   printf("\nEnter filename: ");
   gets(filename);

   /* Write array into a file */
   if ((fileptr = fopen(filename, "w")) == NULL)
   {
      printf("Error: Cannot open file\n");
      exit(0);
   }

   printf("Writing data items to "
          "file %s...\n", filename);
```

continues

Listing 11.11. Continued

```
    fwrite(data, sizeof(data), 1, fileptr);
    fclose(fileptr);          /* Close the file */

    /* Read file into an array */
    if ((fileptr = fopen(filename, "r")) == NULL)
    {   /*  Check return value just to make sure  */
       printf("Error: Cannot open input file\n");
       exit(0);
    }

    printf("Reading data items from file...\n");
    fread(&data2, sizeof(data), 1, fileptr);
    fclose(fileptr);

    printf("The elements of the array are \n");
    for (count=0; count < ITEMS; count++)
    {
       printf("Element %d is %d\n",
               count, data2[count]);

    }

    return 0;
}
```

Sample output of the program looks like this:

```
Enter filename: c:\temp\numbers.dat
Writing data items to file c:\temp\numbers.dat...
Reading data items from file...
The elements of the array are
Element 0 is 8
Element 1 is 57
Element 2 is 5
Element 3 is 309
Element 4 is 33
Element 5 is 87
Element 6 is 55
```

The program stores an array of seven elements into a user-specified disk file. It then reads them back into a separate file and displays the elements on-screen.

You could have written the data elements one at a time using formatted output (with the `fprintf()` function), however writing the whole array out to disk with one statement is much more efficient. Not only does it take less space, it is also faster to load and save the array.

Summary

Disk file input and output is an important part of any program. In this chapter, you learned how to access files in a variety of ways, including both sequential and random-access file I/O. The following important points were covered:

- Before you can access a file, you must use the `fopen()` *function* to gain access to the specific file. In the call to the function, you specify the filename and the mode in which you want to access the file. The `fclose()` *function* is used to close a disk file after it has been opened.

- Every file has an *end-of-file (EOF) marker* attached at the its end. Your program can use this marker to indicate when it has reached the end of the file. The `feof()` function returns a value that informs you if the EOF marker has been reached.

- The `FILE` *pointer* stores essential information about the location and offset of a data file.

- *Character-file I/O* enables you to read or write a single character of information from a disk file.

- The *string I/O functions* enable you to read or write an entire line of text from your disk files at once. The *formatted I/O functions* enable you to create data files that create both alphabetic characters and numeric text.

- *Random-access file input and output* enables you to access any byte of information in a file without having to read in any of the previous file contents. You can instantly go to any location on the disk.

- By storing information in binary format, file I/O is more efficient because memory is conserved and the read and write operations are quicker.

- The two main functions that allow a program to use random access file I/O are `fseek()` *and* `ftell()`. The `fseek()` function moves to any specific location in a file. The `ftell()` function returns the current location in the file.

- A specific number of bytes of data can be written to disk at once with the `fwrite()` *function.* This function enables you to save an entire data structure or array with a single statement. Once you write out a number of bytes to disk with the `fwrite()` function, you can read that data back in with the `fread()` function. The `fread()` *function* reads in a specified number of bytes into a buffer.

INDEX

Symbols

A

I

K

L

W–Z